WINNING
WEIGHT
TRAINING
FOR GIRLS

WINNING WEIGHT TRAINING
FOR GIRLS

DAVID PORTER

Foreword by
GERARD K. GREEN, C.S.C.S., M.B.A.
Rider University

A MOUNTAIN LION BOOK

☑®
Facts On File, Inc.

WINNING WEIGHT TRAINING FOR GIRLS

Facts On File, Inc.
132 West 31st Street
New York NY 10001

Library of Congress Cataloging-in-Publication Data

Porter, David L., 1960–
    Winning weight training for girls / David Porter; foreword by
Gerard K. Green.
        p. cm.
    "A Mountain Lion Book."
    Includes bibliographical references and index.
    ISBN 0-8160-5185-2 (HC)
    1. Weight training for women. 2. Physical fitness for women. I. Title.
    GV546.6.W64P65 2003
    613.7′1′082—dc21   2003003500

Facts On File books are available at special discounts when purchased in bulk quantities for businesses, associations, institutions, or sales promotions. Please call our Special Sales Department in New York at (212) 967-8800 or (800) 322-8755.

You can find Facts On File on the World Wide Web at
http://www.factsonfile.com

Text design by Erika K. Arroyo
Cover design by Nora Wertz

Printed in the United States of America

VB FOF 10 9 8 7 6 5 4 3 2 1

This book is printed on acid-free paper.

For my wonderful wife and best friend, Melody, and for the loves of my life, Gerry Jr., Kaitlyn, and Timothy.

—Gerard K. Green

CONTENTS

FOREWORD

In the many years I have been involved in sports as an athlete and as a strength and conditioning trainer for athletes and nonathletes, one of the trends I have watched develop is the expansion of weight-training programs for male and female athletes in all sports. It used to be that most of the weight training at the college level was done by the football and wrestling teams; now, nearly all teams have strength and conditioning programs that involve weight-training exercises very much like the ones described in this book.

At any level of competition, weight training conducted in a controlled, supervised environment can have many benefits for athletes. It goes without saying that the athlete who is stronger, faster, and more explosive will be more competitive than the athlete who is not, and that when faced with a choice, a coach is more likely to pick the former girl over the latter. In addition, the better-trained athlete will have an advantage in making the transition from high school to college sports, which can be a significant adjustment.

Unfortunately, many high schools do not have the personnel or resources to offer organized weight-training programs for all sports. Some athletes may not stick with a weight-training program because they don't think it is worth the investment of time. If you plan to play sports in college, this can put you at a disadvantage when you are asked to train alongside returning athletes who already have a strength and conditioning foundation. This can result in injury or overtraining as you struggle to make up the difference.

The goal of *Winning Weight Training for Girls* is to provide you with the basis for improving your overall conditioning and performance, whatever sport you play. The programs are set up to follow a progression, beginning with a basic Functional Strength program that gets your joints, bones, and muscles ready for more advanced or isolating resistance exercises, moving on to a Preparatory program that starts you using weights, then to Hypertrophy, Strength and Power programs, and finally to programs tailored to specific sports.

Since no two athletes are at the exact same level of development and conditioning, you may find that you do not have to start at the very beginning of the Functional Strength program. However, keep in mind that sound reasoning and experience drive the design of these programs. Your body can handle only so much stress on the muscles, bones, and ligaments before it will break down; consequently, you should not do too much too soon by skipping parts of the program. To use a math analogy, that would be like somebody trying to do calculus without first learning algebra.

By the same token, your body adapts well to variation, which is the basic idea behind periodization, a concept that is discussed in detail in this book. Periodization in weight training helps you to avoid becoming stale or overtrained, and helps you avoid plateaus where you are not progressing even though you continue to train. Even elite athletes go through phases when they lose some of their motivation.

For beginners, this can occur early in a training cycle, as muscles get sore and it is difficult to see signs of increased strength, speed, and agility. One way you can conquer this is to do what I do with athletes at Rider, which is to test for strength as well as for things like speed or vertical leap before starting the program in the off-season and preseason, and then retest after several weeks of training. If everything is done properly and in the right progression for the particular athlete, improvements will occur. Try this for yourself to see if you are getting positive results. If you are like most athletes, you're goal-oriented. Once you see that you are progressing toward your goal of increasing your strength and conditioning level, you will feel more motivated.

Above all, remember that like any sport, weight training should be fun. You may have to persevere early on, as your body gets used to the new demands you are asking of it, but if you stick with it and stay focused, you (and your body) will develop a routine and you will find yourself looking forward to your training days and getting the most out of them. Use the programs and exercises described in *Winning Weight Training for Girls* as guidelines to help you challenge yourself to be better, and to give yourself an edge in making the team, helping your team become more competitive, and making it to the next level.

Gerard K. Green, C.S.C.S., M.B.A., a strength and conditioning specialist certified by the National Strength and Conditioning Association, has been a strength and conditioning consultant to men's and women's athletic teams at Rider University, in Lawrenceville, N.J., since 1987. He owns a bachelor of science degree in health and physical education from West Chester University, in Pennsylvania.

INTRODUCTION

Over the years, increasing numbers of young athletes have turned to weight training to enhance their training in their specific sports. Yet some of the stereotypes about weights and weight lifting prevail. In particular, the idea of young women increasing their muscle size and strength is still taboo in some quarters, even in the new millennium.

The reality, however, is that athletes of both sexes can derive numerous benefits from weight training, whether they are doing it as part of an overall training program or as an end in itself. Beyond that, the continuous raising of the quality of women's sports—not to mention the competition for college scholarships—makes it almost a requirement that athletes use all resources at their disposal to become the best they can be.

Some of the benefits of weight training are obvious. Numerous studies have shown that an athlete who has engaged in a weight-training program is less likely to sustain injuries than an athlete who has done no strength training—one-third as likely, according to one study—and the rehabilitation time for the weight-trained athlete will be shorter as well. Improved performance often can be directly related to increased strength and coordination, largely because in addition to making your muscles stronger, the type of weight-training programs described in this book improve the way your muscles interact with each other, which affects things like balance and coordination.

Other benefits are not as easily noticeable, but are important nonetheless. Weight training has been shown to:

- Enhance cardiovascular health by decreasing the resting heart rate and blood pressure, and improving blood lipid and lipoprotein levels. It also can improve glucose tolerance in athletes with diabetes mellitus
- Increase lean body mass and produce modest decreases in the relative percentage of body fat
- Increase bone density, which can slow the development of osteoporosis

- Reduce anxiety or depression and improve general psychological well-being
- Improve discipline and concentration
- Reduce stress on your body's systems as a whole

In addition, studies have shown that athletes who do weight training have a higher degree of aerobic power—measured by VO_2max, or maximal oxygen uptake—than do nonathletes, even if they do not perform any aerobic or endurance exercises.

The social aspects of weight training should not be underestimated, either. Many coaches have found that off-season weight programs are a way to promote team unity and camaraderie, as teammates support and encourage one another and motivate one another to stretch their limits.

Female Athletes and Body Image

A big part of self-image comes from how a person views her body versus how society views her body. For female athletes, this can create a dilemma, as social pressures to "look feminine" clash with the need to maintain strength and conditioning for sports. In addition, many women balk at the idea of becoming "too muscular."

To address the latter point, studies have shown that women do not have the same capacity for increasing the size of their muscles as men do. However, women do have almost as much capacity to gain muscle strength proportionally as men, though this will not manifest itself visually since women have a higher percentage of body fat than men.

There are exceptions, of course. Female bodybuilders who train at high levels for extended periods of time can develop larger muscles, especially if they use anabolic steroids, which are basically synthetic versions of male hormones—and which are banned by most, if not all, amateur and professional sports organizations.

A well-planned weight-training program like the ones described in this book will give you the best chance of improving your athletic performance as well as giving you a stronger, healthier-looking physique—without making you look like Arnold Schwarzenegger.

Winning Weight Training for Girls begins with a basic overview of how your muscles work and how they adapt to weight-training exercises, takes you through the steps of getting started and avoiding injury, and then introduces periodization, the method of training that has been adapted by elite and Olympic athletes. The next several sections feature sample periodized training programs, starting with a general program to develop basic strength and coordination and followed by programs tailored to specific sports.

These programs are specifically designed to increase muscle strength and size as well as develop coordination. They use a variety of weights, weight machines, and other apparatus, some of which may not be available at your school or gym. If this is the case, consult with your coach or trainer about ways to substitute other exercises.

There are many references in this book to precautions and safety when using weights and learning new exercises. These cannot be stressed enough, as the number one cause of injuries to weight lifters is poor technique and improper supervision. Particularly if you are using free weights, you should never perform these exercises on your own, or with weight that seems too heavy for you. Always learn the exercises from a qualified instructor, and start with light weights until you have mastered the technique and are ready to increase the intensity of your workout.

Weight training is not a quick fix; you will only realize gains in strength and power over time. Too many athletes try to do too much too soon, and wind up injuring themselves or getting frustrated. It is better to give yourself enough time to go slowly and then gradually build up to a high level of intensity, as this will guarantee progress and help you avoid hitting a plateau.

The other thing to remember is that weight training alone will not make you a better athlete. You'll notice as you read through the programs in this book that many exercises combine weights with exercises called plyometrics, which use explosive movements such as jumping, bounding, and medicine ball drills to get your muscles used to reaching maximal strength in as short a time as possible. These exercises are characterized by an accelerated movement that follows a decelerated motion, and they have varying degrees of difficulty and stress to the body that could cause injury if not done properly. They require a foundation of strength and good technique, and should only be done under supervision. Other exercises focus on agility, and if you are playing on a team your coach will have you spend significant time on these exercises as part of your overall conditioning program.

1

HOW YOUR MUSCLES ADAPT TO WEIGHT TRAINING

HOW YOUR MUSCLES WORK

To understand how weight training prepares your muscles for the specific movements required in each sport, it is helpful to understand how your muscles work—what they are made of, how they work together, and how they adapt to stress caused by resistance exercises.

Your muscles do not actually exert any force on objects by themselves. Muscles are attached to bones by tendons, and when a muscle contracts—which is what it does when it lifts weights or exerts force against another object—the muscle fibers contract, thus pulling on tendons. This moves the bones that rotate around the various joints in your body. You have three types of joints: uniaxial joints, which act like hinges (your elbow, for example); biaxial joints, which allow two types of movement (your wrist and ankle), and multiaxial joints which allow three types of movements. Your shoulder, hip, and knee are multiaxial joints.

Muscles are made up of thousands of cells called muscle fibers. These are held together with tissue and attached to your bones by tendons. The muscle fibers are innervated, or stimulated to action, by motor nerves that can control as few as one or as many as several hundred muscle fibers. The nerve-muscle combination is called a motor unit. The muscle fibers become excited when the nerves send a signal to the muscle in the form of an electric current that causes the release of acetylcholine, a chemical that causes the muscle fiber to contract. This action is called a twitch.

1

Muscle fibers are commonly classified as slow-twitch or fast-twitch. Fast-twitch muscle fibers develop force quickly and over a short period of time, while slow-twitch muscle fibers develop force more slowly but over a longer period of time. Not surprisingly, slow-twitch muscle fibers are what give you endurance and energy during, say, a road race; fast-twitch muscle fibers, on the other hand, are what allow you to sprint at full speed or perform other actions that are explosive but short in duration. Your muscles contain slow- and fast-twitch muscle fibers in varying proportions.

EFFECTS OF RESISTANCE TRAINING

When you lift weights or do other kinds of resistance training, you are increasing the size of your muscle fibers, a process known as hypertrophy. This helps you increase your strength. Interestingly, some studies have shown that fast-twitch muscle fibers show greater increases in size than slow-twitch fibers; this means that athletes with a higher percentage of fast-twitch fibers may have an advantage when it comes to resistance training. It also may explain why different athletes will increase muscle size in different proportions even if they are performing the same training program. Muscle-fiber increase from resistance training has been shown to be comparable in women and men, though often it is not as noticeable because women have a higher percentage of body fat than men, along with fewer hormones that help increase muscle size.

When you begin a weight-training program like the ones described in this book, it generally takes your body about four to six weeks to adapt to the new stresses, which means you need to be patient as you strengthen your muscles, ligaments, and bones. Neurologically, your body makes these adaptations before your muscles, bones, and ligaments do. So, you may be able to increase your strength within the first two weeks or so because your neurological system is making a quicker adaptation and you are developing coordination. But for the actual strength of the muscles, ligaments, and bones, the benefits do not occur until a little bit later. Also, you may not notice an increase in muscle size (hypertrophy) for the first month or two, even though you can feel yourself getting stronger.

If you max out with the same set and rep scheme too early, you could accomplish strength initially, but then you would hit a plateau and not progress past that level. Using a periodized training program, it will take longer to hit plateaus, but those plateaus will be higher, and you will be able to progress past them by following the periodization process. So, you should keep in mind that the program will get you where you want to go, even if your friend at the gym who is using a different program (or none at all) may be lifting more weight than you are in the early stages. Programs using periodization have been scientifically proven to show better results over the long term.

ENDURANCE TRAINING VERSUS RESISTANCE TRAINING

Though this book focuses on resistance training, endurance training is a vital part of a training program for many athletes, from distance runners to swimmers to soccer players to basketball players. Most sports require a combination of short, explosive motions (**anaerobic fitness**) and longer, more controlled motions (**aerobic fitness**).

The effects of these two types of training on overall strength and endurance should be considered. Studies have shown that resistance training will not improve your muscles' aerobic capacity, but nor does it decrease it, either. In fact, resistance training may improve short-term muscle endurance for athletes such as cyclists or distance runners.

Endurance training, meanwhile, will increase your aerobic capacity but will not increase strength, and in many cases will actually decrease strength. For example, if a sprinter only trains by jogging a few miles a day rather than running sprints, she will gradually lose the fast-twitch muscle fiber development that enables her to sprint at high speeds.

Depending on the sport you play and your overall conditioning goals, then, you will most likely incorporate aspects of resistance and endurance training into your program. If you are a soccer player, for example, your team practices probably include aerobic (jogging laps) and anaerobic (wind sprints) activities.

2
PRINCIPLES OF WEIGHT TRAINING

Everyone knows that lifting weights will make you stronger. But how is this best accomplished? Like any other activity, there are basic principles of weight training that answer this and other questions, and provide guidelines for athletes starting out on a weight-training program.

OVERLOADING

Overloading is the basic principle of resistance training. In simple terms, it is the act of forcing your muscles to do more than they are used to doing. This is what enables you to increase your muscle size and strength. You can achieve the overload effect by increasing the amount of weight you are lifting, or by lifting the same amount more times than you did before. For instance, if you normally do three sets of 10 repetitions at 80 pounds in a bench press, you could overload the muscles by doing an extra set or two; or, you could do three sets of seven repetitions at 100 pounds.

Overloading is not just a method to increase your muscle size; it is the only accepted method. If you reach a point where you can easily do three sets of, say, 80 pounds and you do not increase that weight or the number of times you are lifting it, you will hit a plateau and will stop progressing. The training programs described in this book are designed to constantly adapt so that you continue to overload your muscles and increase your muscle capacity.

WHAT IS SPECIFICITY?

While everybody's general goal when taking part in weight training is to make improvements in muscle size, strength, and power (or any combination of those), athletes must focus their training so that these improvements are directly related to the sport(s) they play. For instance, a distance runner is not going to benefit from the same exercises as a sprinter, nor will a competitive basketball player need to develop the same specific muscle groups as a swimmer.

There are a few ways to add specificity to your training: You can train specific muscle groups; you can train for speed as opposed to strength, which means using lighter weights but moving them at a faster velocity; and you can use dynamic (moving) or isometric (stationary) muscle actions. Dynamic muscle actions are the ones that occur when you raise a weight (concentric action) and bring it back down (eccentric action). Isometric muscle actions occur when you push against an immovable object.

Concentric muscle actions (shortening of the muscles) are what produce power and motion in an athlete, while eccentric muscle actions (lengthening of the muscles) aid in decelerating the body—think about when you come to a quick stop while you are running. Isometric muscle actions are important in sports like wrestling.

VARIATION

There are many variables in any weight-training program, which means there are many ways to add variety to your workouts by making slight changes to some of those variables. You can alter the intensity of your workouts over the course of a week or a month by increasing or decreasing the amount of weight and the number of repetitions. This is one of the staples of periodized training, which is covered in detail in a later chapter. You can also substitute different exercises for the ones you are doing. You can change the way you do certain exercises, such as changing your grip on a barbell, though this should only be done under supervision to avoid risking injury. You can increase or decrease the length and amount of your rest breaks. All of these subtle changes will help you avoid getting stale or reaching a plateau in your training.

IMPORTANCE OF REST

Once you have started a weight-training program, the length and frequency of the rest periods you take is almost as important as the number of sets and reps you are doing in your workout. Why is this so? In addition to allowing you to recover from the muscle overload your body experiences when you are training, rest actually enables you to adapt to the new stress and bounce back even stronger. So, while you are sweating in the gym and telling yourself that you are building muscle and gaining strength, most of the actual physiological changes in your body are actually happening between workouts, on your off days.

Some training programs purposely restrict the amount of rest during a short period and then follow that with a similar period of less intense training. But in general, you should take at least 24 to 48 hours between training sessions to allow your body to adapt. During this period and during your training program as a whole, it is also crucial to eat a balanced diet and, especially, to get enough sleep. Believe it or not, your body adapts to the stresses of training while you are sleeping.

INDIVIDUALIZATION

Every athlete brings unique experiences, goals, and abilities to a team and to a training program. More important, she brings a body with unique characteristics that affect how she trains and how she should train. This is why it is necessary to get a full physical examination before undergoing any weight-training program, and to make sure your doctor notifies your trainer of your medical history as it relates to your training activities.

A previous injury or condition will affect which exercises you do— or which ones you avoid—and how you do them. For instance, there is a whole set of exercises designed specifically to rehabilitate each type of knee injury. If you are recovering from an injury or just have weakness or laxity (looseness) in any of your joints, you need to make sure whoever is supervising your weight-training program is aware of this and can adjust your program accordingly.

DETRAINING

It certainly is not front-page news that ceasing training will gradually chip away at any gains you have made. But it is interesting to note that studies have shown that a break of one or two weeks in which no training is performed will not cause a significant loss of strength, particularly if the break is preceded by an intense period of training. The break has the effect of rejuvenating you so that you are ready to resume training again.

This is the general idea behind athletes easing off on their training, or "tapering," as a major competition approaches. This way they are fresh for the competition but their overall physical condition has not suffered.

WEIGHT MACHINES VERSUS FREE WEIGHTS

This is one of the eternal questions encountered in resistance training. It might be irrelevant for you if your school or gym only has one or the other. Either way, it is useful to consider some of the advantages and disadvantages of using weight machines, such as Nautilus, Universal, or other brands, and "free weights," which essentially consist of dumbbells and barbells to which you add or subtract metal plates.

Weight machines:

- allow greater control over the weight, and therefore decrease the risk of injury
- offer different types of resistance, depending on the model
- make it easier to add or subtract weight or move from one exercise to another
- do not require as much technique training as free weights

but also:

- are far more expensive to buy and maintain than free weights
- offer a limited number of exercises
- use less range of motion than free weights

Free weights, meanwhile:

- are cheaper to buy and maintain than weight machines
- offer exercises that require coordination of several muscle groups and more closely mirror the motions you make in various sports
- use more range of motion than weight machines
- give a greater benefit for the entire body by forcing you to use some muscles as stabilizers while you perform exercises

but also:

- require more technique training than weight machines
- offer less control over the weights, thus increasing the chance of injury
- require spotters for many exercises
- cause more clutter than weight machines

OTHER TYPES OF RESISTANCE

Though the majority of exercises described in this book involve weights that you push against the force of gravity, other types of resistance can be used to develop strength and power. Ask your trainer or coach about these other methods and whether they should be incorporated into your training program.

Friction

Some types of exercise machines use friction, which is resistance caused by two objects rubbing together, to accomplish training goals. Some cycling machines and wrist-curl devices fall under this category. In general, you have to use more force at the outset of these exercises and then a lower, constant amount of force to maintain the exercise motion.

Fluid Resistance

Hydraulic and pneumatic exercise machines—ones that use cylinders and pistons rather than traditional weights—are designed to mirror the resistance you encounter in sports like swimming, sprinting, baseball (pitching, specifically), and others, even though, except for swimming, the resistance is actually provided by the air. Exercises using these machines tend to limit the amount of force you can exert on the weight, particularly as you move through the exercise, so that if you are doing a bench press it feels like you are working harder the closer your arms get to a fully extended position. Fluid-resistance exercises do not really require any eccentric muscle action, and so may not be the best exercises for athletes who want to improve their running and jumping ability.

Elasticity

Many home gym units use a system of springs or rubber bands to provide resistance. These exercises provide low resistance at the beginning of the motion and high resistance toward the end. This can be problematic because your muscles work in the opposite manner; which is to say, they are capable of exerting more force at the beginning of a range of motion and less at the end.

PLYOMETRIC TRAINING

The training programs described in this book contain exercises that are not technically considered resistance exercises because they do not involve weights. These exercises, called plyometric exercises, train your balance and coordination as well as your muscles' ability to accelerate and decelerate quickly. Plyometric exercises improve explosiveness and reaction time by manipulation of the stretch reflex. Plyometrics is relatively new, but it has become popular because it focuses on exercises that simulate specific motions performed in different sports.

Some examples of plyometric exercises can be found in the Power phases of the specific sport programs. For instance, one of the exercises in the Softball Power phase requires you to do a squat using a weighted barbell, then follow it with squat jumps, in which you elevate and land from a squatting position. This type of complex exercise combines resistance (the squat) with an explosive movement (the squat jump) to both strengthen your muscles and prepare them for the movements required in competition. Jumping rope is another example of a low-level plyometric exercise.

Perhaps even more so than with training involving weights, plyometric exercises should always be learned and performed under the supervision of qualified trainers or coaches, and with equipment that is in good condition and is appropriate to the exercise being attempted.

STRENGTH VERSUS POWER

"Strength" and "power" are not considered the same thing, though many people equate the two. Strength is force, or the ability to exert enough force on an object to put it into motion at any speed. Power, however, is the rate of force (force times speed), or how fast you can move an object. This becomes important when you look at what type of training you need to do for your specific sport. For example, in addition to utilizing power, a wrestler also needs to develop the strength to push against a heavy object—another wrestler—while a volleyball player needs to develop power that will enable her to propel the ball with a faster motion or jump explosively to make a block. (See the discussion earlier in this book about the difference between slow-twitch and fast-twitch muscles.)

Determining strength can be a tricky endeavor, but studies have shown that if two athletes of different height and weight but similar levels of body fat have biceps of the same circumference, their biceps will have approximately the same amount of strength. Though the taller, heavier athlete in this example would by design have more total muscle mass in her biceps, the shorter, lighter athlete would have a higher strength-to-mass ratio and would probably be better able to propel herself and accelerate rapidly.

TRAINING FOR POWER

Training for power is important for all athletes who play sports that require explosive movements, or that involve moving an object at great speed, such as balls, bats, or sticks. To review, power is the rate of force (force times speed), or how fast you are able to move an object. Strength, by contrast, is the ability to exert enough force on an object to put it into motion.

The type of training exercises you can do will naturally be dictated by the type of equipment you have access to; however, it is generally agreed that power exercises are best performed using free weights and using what are called Olympic-style lifts. Some of these lifts include snatches, power cleans, and hang cleans, which are described elsewhere in this book. They are considered more efficient exercises because:

- they use a wider range of motion and involve most of your body's muscles on each lift
- they require timing, coordination, and balance
- they require actions that more closely approximate the movements required in competitive sports

Another example of exercises that develop power are exercises that use a medicine ball, which are featured in the programs described in this book. These exercises require a high level of intensity at velocities that mimic the speed of a sport-specific movement without putting undue stress on your lower back, and are a good way to break up a workout in the weight room.

Remember that if your sport requires explosive movements, you have to train accordingly. Developing individual body parts—your biceps or back muscles, for instance—will not translate to improved performance, nor will training with weights in a slow, steady manner improve your muscles' ability to fire explosively. To increase power, your goal should be to produce maximum strength in the shortest time possible. Think of a sprinter, whose foot is touching the ground for about one-tenth of a second on each stride. Her muscles have about half that time to prepare to push off and propel her forward.

3

GETTING STARTED

GETTING A CHECKUP

Your school will most likely require that you undergo a complete physical examination before you are allowed to compete on a school-sponsored team, but you should also get a full checkup before embarking on any weight-training program, even during the off-season. This is so your coach or trainer is aware of any existing conditions you have that might affect your choice of exercises. These can be anything. You may have Osgood Schlatter's, a knee condition that affects young athletes; or you may have fallen off a horse when you were younger and injured your shoulder; or you may have asthma or some other condition. In any case, it is crucial that your coach or trainer knows your relevant medical history.

WARMING UP AND COOLING DOWN

A warmup should be a part of your routine whenever you are getting ready to practice or play sports, but it should also precede any weight-training session. When you train with weights, you are asking your body's joints, ligaments, and muscles to handle more stress than they are used to. In order to do this efficiently, you need to raise your body's core temperature so that blood is flowing to the areas that will be handling the stress.

Your warmup should be in two parts. Typically, you should do a general warmup such as a cardiovascular exercise—light jogging on a treadmill, jumping rope for a few minutes, riding an exercise bike—

just to start to sweat and get your heart pumping and your blood circulating. Then do some stretching exercises to get range of motion, and then do a specific warmup for the specific activity. If you do not warm up correctly, you increase your chances of suffering an injury.

For an example of a specific warmup, if you are doing a bench press, you might do some push-ups or do some bench presses using half the weight you are going to be lifting during the program. This lets those muscles and bones and ligaments know what is ahead for them. For a warmup set, you would generally use half the weight you would normally use in the exercise. Particularly when you get into higher weights, such as when you are doing 100 percent of your **repetition maximum (RM)** for four or six repetitions, that is a lot of weight and your muscles and joints need to be ready.

Cooling down is no less important than warming up. Whatever activity you are engaged in, you need to take adequate time to let your body make the transition from being stressed to being at rest. There is a physiological reason for this: Intense anaerobic activities such as sprinting or weight training cause the buildup of lactic acid in your muscles, which contributes to muscle fatigue. To help your muscles remove some of the lactic acid buildup after a strenuous workout, it often helps to jog, skip rope, or perform some other type of low-intensity exercise for five or 10 minutes (competitive wrestlers are often seen doing this after a match).

MANAGING PAIN

The phrase "no pain, no gain" has become ingrained in our culture, and there is a measure of truth contained in those words. The key thing to remember, though, is not to take it too seriously and push yourself too far. If you are embarking on a weight-training program, and if you stick to it and take it seriously, there are bound to be times when you will experience soreness and muscle pain. Since no one can "feel your pain," it is up to you to listen to your body when it is giving you signals.

Though you will start your program gradually and slowly increase the intensity of your workouts, you may find that you become fatigued by the end of your workout, and are sore the next day. This is normal, and it is your body's way of adapting to the new stresses being placed upon it. The question is, when is it soreness and when is it a sign of an injury? You should communicate with your trainer or coach if you are experiencing anything more than light stiffness on the day after a workout, particularly in the early days and weeks of the program. He or she will probably ask you if you can move the affected area in a normal range of motion, or if you are experiencing any weakness. This is not the time to be a hero—untreated injuries only become worse!

For general soreness—which you are guaranteed to experience the day after your first workout—it often is wise to pull back a little and adjust your intensity. For example, if you did one set of several exercises during the first workout and had a low degree of stiffness, you would probably do one set again the second workout. If you did one set the first day and didn't feel anything, you might do two sets the second day. If you felt very sore after the first day, however, you would probably wait until the soreness went away before resuming, and even then probably lower the amount of weight a little bit. Obviously, it is important to let your coach or trainer know what level of muscle soreness you are experiencing.

OVERTRAINING

Similarly, you may reach a point where you feel fatigued regularly. This is common among athletes who push themselves hard (which is what all good athletes do, anyway). This is where the "no pain, no gain" theory can lead you into trouble. You may be able to push your body to go those extra few laps on the track or in the pool, but when you are doing resistance training you may be sabotaging your training and your health by doing this, as fatigue causes a breakdown in technique which can lead to injury. At the very least, you will not be getting as much out of your workout. When your body is fatigued and you are asking it to do more, something is going to shut down. This is known as "overtraining."

Overtraining is often hard to detect because it manifests itself in ways other than just sore muscles. Here are some of the telltale signs of overtraining:

- Inability to sleep
- Mood swings
- Altered eating habits
- Muscle fatigue and soreness
- Depression or lack of motivation
- Frequent illnesses

If you notice any of these symptoms, consult your coach or trainer and, in concert with them, take a hard look at your training schedule and seriously consider taking some extra rest between workouts. You will lose a negligible amount of the gains you have already made if you take two or three days off between workouts instead of one, and it may help you return with a new attitude.

WHAT TO WEAR

For the most part, what you wear when you are training with weights is mostly the same as what you would wear when you are playing your sport or doing other exercises. However, there are some general guidelines and some specific gear that can enhance your weight-training program.

Clothing

Your normal exercise wear will usually do unless you want to have more support for your muscles and joints, in which case you may want to wear clothing that is made of expandable material. A general rule is to not wear baggy tops or bottoms that can get in the way of weights or machinery.

Shoes

Always wear shoes when you are in a weight room, unless you fancy a broken toe from someone inadvertently dropping a weight on it. Special weight-lifting shoes manufactured by the major shoe manufacturers give you good balance and support, but you can use any type of cross-training shoe that offers lateral support. You may want to save your running shoes for running, as their wider and raised soles can make it easier to roll your ankle to the outside.

Gloves

Specially designed weight-lifting gloves can protect your hands from chafing and callusing that can result from continuous grasping of barbells and dumbbells. Ask your coach or trainer to recommend some brands.

Belts

Weight-lifting belts are used by competitive powerlifters, but they can be useful for athletes at all levels, too, as they can help support your abdominal muscles and lower back when you are lifting heavy weights. This can be particularly helpful when you are doing squats, hex bar dead lifts, and Olympic-type exercises, for example. They are not necessary for exercises that do not place stress on your back. Check with your coach or trainer about trying a weight belt—but remember that proper technique is the best safeguard against injury.

Braces and Supports

These are used most often to allow athletes to continue to train while recovering from a joint or muscle injury. Braces, which frequently feature hard plastic or metal hinges, allow less range of motion and typically are used after an acute injury. Supports, which can consist of padding, wraps, or other softer materials, allow more range of motion and help to compress the affected area and keep it warm. They can also cause discomfort and even injury if they are too tight, however. Needless to say, you should always consult your physician or orthopedist before you attempt to return to weight training after suffering an injury.

4

SAFETY AND AVOIDING INJURY

Believe it or not, it may be easier to get injured in the weight room than on the playing field. Why is this so? Consider that you could run around for an hour and a half playing soccer or basketball or hockey, and not put the same stress on a particular muscle or muscle group that you are going to get from 10 repetitions of a weight-training exercise. The basic idea of weight training is that you are isolating and overloading a muscle, which puts a lot of stress on it. The end result is positive, but the flip side is that you have to be cautious about how you proceed so that you do not increase your risk of injury.

IMPORTANCE OF TECHNIQUE

Using proper technique is one of the most basic ways of avoiding injury. It should go without saying that you should never attempt any unfamiliar exercise without first learning the right technique from a qualified coach or trainer. This holds true for familiar exercises as well; many athletes may think they know how to perform a particular exercise but in fact are doing it incorrectly, which increases the risk of injury. Technique is one area in which it always pays to cheat to the side of caution.

Sometimes a seemingly small change in technique can make a big difference in how your muscles respond to a particular exercise. For example, when you are doing an exercise called a squat, slightly changing the angle of your torso to the floor can shift some of the stress from your knees and quadriceps (thigh muscles) to your hips and hamstrings.

The Exercises section of this book describes techniques for all the exercises contained in the various sample programs. It cannot be stressed enough that these techniques should be practiced under the supervision of your trainer or coach, and that spotters be used wherever noted.

AVOIDING MUSCLE IMBALANCES

Another way you can get injured is from muscle imbalances. This is particularly true for athletes who play one sport year-round. Swimming, tennis, volleyball, basketball . . . whatever the sport, if you focus on it exclusively you are inevitably going to strengthen some muscle groups at the expense of others. This creates a muscle imbalance which can lead to injury if you are performing weight-training exercises that assume you have balanced muscles.

To avoid muscle imbalances, it is generally suggested that you cross-train, which means including different types of activities in your training program. For the purposes of general conditioning this means doing a variety of aerobic activities (biking, swimming, jogging) combined with weight training. For competitive athletes, it can mean soccer players playing some basketball during the off-season to work on their hand-eye coordination and jumping ability. The benefit of playing more than one sport is that you are working different muscles as well as building a combination of strength and endurance.

GENERAL SAFETY TIPS

Techniques and safety tips for all the specific exercises in this book are listed in a separate section. Here are some general rules to remember about weight-training technique:

- All exercises, resistance or nonresistance, should be performed in a controlled, fluid motion rather than an awkward, jerky motion.
- Do at least one warmup set using light weights (about 50 percent of what you will actually be lifting) before you do your actual set, particularly for exercises that place stress on your shoulders or knees. (Although not used in these programs, doing more than one warmup set is OK. If you do this, successive sets would be higher than 50 percent).
- Keep weights close to your body. The further the weight is from your body, the less control you have and the greater likelihood you will suffer an injury.

- If you are turning while pulling or lifting a weight, make sure you turn your whole body instead of twisting only your lower back or hips.
- When you are doing exercises from a standing position, spread your chest and have your shoulders back. You never want to be round-shouldered.
- Keep your back as straight as possible—forcing your back to handle a heavy load when it is in a curved position is a recipe for a back injury. For certain lifts, such as dead lifts, some athletes arch their backs, but this can be risky as well. In general, your back should be straight or have its normal arch, and not have a bend at all.
- When you are performing any exercises with free weights, remember to bend your knees slightly, as this will take some of the pressure off your lower back.
- Always start out with a lighter weight when you are learning a new exercise or returning from a one- or two-week layoff.
- Do not hold your breath when you are lifting weights. A good rule of thumb to follow is to exhale on the initial thrust of the exercise (pushing the bench press bar upward, for example) and inhale on the second part of the motion.
- A general phrase to remember when you are doing resistance training exercises is "start fast, end slow." When you are doing a bench press, for example, you want to take about two seconds to push the weight upward, then about twice as long bringing the weight back down. Your muscles shorten during the first half of the motion (concentric) and lengthen during the downward motion (eccentric). You will get more benefit if you go slowly during the eccentric part of the motion.
- Your shoulders are particularly susceptible to injury during resistance training, due to the inherent looseness of the joint and the fact that they are often asked to lift heavy weights. Always make sure you are warmed up and use proper technique when you are doing bench presses, incline presses, and lat pulls. Bench presses in particular place stress on your shoulders, and should be performed no more than once per week.

Most people can withstand more resistance on the negative (eccentrically) than on the positive. For example, if you are unable to do regular pull-ups, you can do a modified version where you start in the finished position while standing on a box or weight bench, and then just let yourself down slowly. This is a way to strengthen your muscles so you are eventually strong enough to perform the complete exercise.

WEIGHT TRAINING AND THE YOUNG ATHLETE

Many studies have examined the effect of weight training on athletes in their early teens whose bones and cartilage are not fully developed. While these studies found that injuries to adolescent weight lifters occurred at about the same rate as to adults, they also recognize that younger athletes have unique concerns. For example, if you are experiencing a growth spurt, you may have decreased flexibility as your muscles and tendons adapt to the changes and "catch up." Also, there is the possibility of damage to growth cartilage plates, which are located at the end of the bones around your joints. Young baseball or softball pitchers are at risk for this type of injury from the repeated stress of throwing a ball.

Tellingly, studies have shown that the chief cause of injuries to adolescents from weight training is improper technique in an unsupervised setting, often involving lifting too much weight. This only reinforces the rule that you should never attempt an exercise unless you have mastered the technique, and should always do so under the supervision of a qualified coach or trainer, preferably one who is familiar with weight-training programs for younger athletes.

SAFETY AT THE GYM

With more and more athletes taking part in weight training, the number of related injuries is rising. As noted above, the majority of these injuries result from improper technique and lack of proper supervision. This does not necessarily mean, however, that the majority of these injuries occur in the home. A gym or health club, while providing the machines and other apparatus you need to do your workout, can be potentially as treacherous as your home gym.

To address the issue of safety at the gym, the National Strength and Conditioning Association (NSCA) created the following guidelines:

1. Supervisors should have mandatory cardiopulmonary resuscitation (CPR) and blood-borne pathogen training as part of their background.
2. For junior high school athletes, the supervisor-athlete ratio should be 1:10; for high school athletes, 1:15; and for college or professional athletes, 1:20.
3. There should be 100 square feet of training space for every athlete using the area at any one time, depending on the type of equipment being used.

4. No more than three athletes at a time should use one barbell or training station.

5. An emergency response plan should be developed, posted, and rehearsed. An emergency phone should be readily accessible at all times.

6. Equipment must be regularly inspected and maintained, with inspection records kept. Damaged equipment should not be used, and should be removed from use until repaired.

7. Signs describing appropriate use and including warnings should be posted for all equipment.

8. All participants should have proper medical clearance and legal waivers before starting training.

9. Strength and conditioning supervisors should have a bachelor's or master's degree from an accredited college or university.

10. Supervisors must be present during all activities, with a clear view of all participants, and close enough to provide assistance or spotting when needed.

11. Exercise machines should be assembled and tested by professionals before they are used in training programs, and should be inspected at regular intervals.

12. The gym environment should be reviewed, including floor surface, lighting, temperature, and ventilation.

13. All equipment should be cleaned and/or disinfected regularly, and athletes should be encouraged to wipe down skin-contact surfaces after use.

14. Strength and conditioning professionals must not prescribe, recommend, or provide drugs, controlled substances, or supplements that are illegal, prohibited, or harmful to athletes for any purpose, including enhancing athletic performance, conditioning, or physique.

5
PERIODIZED TRAINING

THE BASICS

Periodized training, or periodization, is really just a formal-sounding word for a relatively basic concept: a long-term training plan that helps you improve muscle size, strength, and general fitness by varying the intensity of your workouts and alternating specific exercises. It was developed in eastern Europe in the 1950s and 1960s and has been adapted and modified by Western trainers and coaches since then. Olympic athletes have used forms of periodized training since the 1960s.

The general principle of periodized training is that your body responds better to periodic changes in your training program as opposed to doing the same program over and over. In addition, by changing different aspects of your workout—the number of sets and repetitions for each exercise, the type of exercises, the length of rest breaks between exercises—and by following different programs that produce different benefits, it helps to keep your training from becoming stale, which can keep you from reaching a plateau and not progressing any further. For competitive athletes, this translates to peaking at the right time, such as when you are ready to begin a season of competition.

Also, when you are doing the same program and the same exercises all the time, there is an increased chance of injury caused by overuse of specific muscle groups. One of the main principles behind periodization is that increasing and decreasing the intensity of your workouts over the course of a week or several weeks, as well as including adequate rest and recovery, will help your body better adapt to the overload and stress on your muscles and reduce the likelihood of injury. (Contrary to what might seem obvious, most of your body's adapting to this increased stress occurs on the days *between* workouts.)

You can compare it to when you get a scrape or injury from friction that causes a sore. If you let it alone for a while it will scab and then produce a callus, and you can then continually build on that callus. But if you are constantly scraping it and rubbing it, you will not get the same end result.

Studies have shown that periodized training programs are better at increasing strength, power, and lean muscle mass than nonperiodized training programs over a span of weeks or months.

DETERMINING YOUR REPETITION MAXIMUM (RM)

Determining your RM for a particular exercise is an important step that must happen before you can embark on any weight-training program and must be performed in an organized, supervised environment to achieve the best results. It is particularly crucial if you are new to weight training.

Your repetition maximum is the highest number of repetitions you can lift a certain weight. For instance, if you can bench-press 80 pounds 10 times but not 11 times, then your 10-repetition maximum, or 10RM, is 80 pounds. You may be able to lift 100 pounds six times, but no more; this means your 6RM is 100 pounds. These are key numbers to know, because the amount of weight you lift throughout your weight-training program will be a percentage of your RM for each specific exercise.

(Some weight-training programs use your 1RM, which is the maximum amount of weight you can lift one time, as a starting point, but for the purposes of this book we will be using different RMs for different exercises.)

For beginners, one way to determine RMs is to take a three-step approach, as follows:

Step 1 involves basic muscle endurance exercises, such as push-ups, sit-ups, and squat thrusts, to prepare the muscles and establish a basic level of conditioning before moving on to actual lifting.

Step 2 consists of practicing the exercises without using any resistance, perhaps with a wooden dowel in place of a barbell. It is essential that before any actual weights are lifted, technique should be observed and approved by a qualified trainer or coach. It is easy for someone who has never done a squat before to hurt her back, even at a low weight, so it is important to make sure the torso, abdominals, and lower back are strong. For three weeks you would practice doing the squat (and other exercises) three days a week without any weight, before gradually starting to use the barbell.

Step 3 begins the process of determining your RMs. As you should do before all weight-training sessions (and any practices or competition, for that matter), start with a short warmup to get the blood flowing to your muscles and joints. This can consist of jogging on a treadmill, jumping rope, or anything that will help you break a sweat and raise your body temperature. The next step is to do specific warmups for the exercises you will be performing. For example, if you are going to be doing bench presses, you might do 10 push-ups, then rest for 30 to 60 seconds before doing the bench press.

Now you are ready to perform the actual exercises. Using the bench press example, you would probably want to start by doing 10 repetitions using the barbell alone, which weighs about 45 pounds. If this can be accomplished with good technique and without fatigue, you would take a break for a few minutes and move on to do another exercise, such as a low row or leg press, again using the lightest possible weight. Then you would come back to the bench press and, depending on how your first set felt, would add some weight to the bar.

The idea is to find a weight at which you can do about 10 or 12 repetitions. Depending on your general size and strength, you may only want to add a few five-pound weights to the bar before you reach your 10RM or 12RM. The key is to go gradually and add weights until you find the correct level. Having said that, it is obvious that after a certain point, you are going to get diminishing returns as you get more fatigued. For this reason, it is usually best to try and reach your RM on your third set.

To avoid overloading one group of muscles too much, rotate three or four exercises in this manner. Also, make sure to take sufficient recovery time between exercises, usually about three or four minutes. As always, you should perform these exercises in the presence of a coach or trainer who is experienced in weight-training techniques.

After you have figured out your RMs for the different exercises, you usually take a day off, then come back in and do one set of each exercise. Any fine-tuning can be done at this point. Once that is done, you are ready to start your program.

HOW TO VARY YOUR PROGRAM

There is an infinite number of ways to vary your training program, but in order to gain the most benefit you need to make the alterations systematically. This is one of the principles behind periodization. Later in this book, these changes will be described in detail as the various programs are spelled out. First, we will go over the types of changes you can make and what they will add to your training program.

Training Frequency

How often you should train is dictated by a number of variables, among them your general conditioning level, your training goals, what point you have reached during your program, what type of exercises you are performing, and at what intensity you are performing them. Too-infrequent training will not help you reach your goals; too-frequent training can leave you burned out or injured.

In general, it is recommended that you train on alternate days to allow your muscles adequate time to adapt to the new stresses on them. You will notice that this is the format used in the sample programs described in this book. If you are well trained and have already performed resistance training programs, you may benefit from more frequent workouts. For athletes just beginning a weight-training program, it is especially important to get adequate rest between workouts.

You may also find that different muscles have different recovery times. This is sometimes true of upper-body muscles versus lower-body muscles, as the former usually are able to recover more quickly than the latter. By the same token, your muscles will take longer to recover from multiple-joint exercises, which place stress on more than one joint (back squats, dead lifts), then they will from single-joint exercises (biceps curls, knee extensions). Even though professional bodybuilders train daily—or sometimes more than once a day—they frequently focus on single-joint exercises.

If your goals are to maximize your strength and power, you will probably need less frequent workouts at higher intensity, and if you are seeking to increase your muscle size or endurance, you will probably need more workouts but at lower intensity. If you are recovering from an injury or illness, common sense dictates that you should return gradually to your previous level of workout frequency. That is, if you were training three or four days per week before, start with one day the first week, two days the second week, and three days the third week. Ask your coach or trainer for advice, and remember always to err on the side of caution when dealing with injuries or illness.

Number of Repetitions

In general, a low number of repetitions (2–6) of a higher weight will increase muscular strength, while a higher number of repetitions (6–12) at a lower weight will increase muscular size. Higher numbers of repetitions (13–20) at even lower weights will increase your muscular endurance.

Training Intensity

Throughout this book there are references to training intensity, which is basically another way to describe how much weight, or load, you are lifting. As noted in an earlier section, power is defined as the rate of force (force times speed), or how fast you are able to move an object of a certain weight. Intensity is defined as the power output of an exercise, which is based on both the amount of weight and the speed at which you move it.

You will see in the sample weight-training programs described in this book that each exercise is done using a percentage of your repetition maximum (RM), which is the maximum number of repetitions you can perform at a certain weight. This is an easy way to measure the intensity of your workout. During the early weeks of the Hypertrophy phase of the Basketball training program, for example, you will be performing exercises at 85–90 percent of your RM. During the more intense weeks of the program, you will be using weights at 95–100 percent of your RM.

Even though you won't be lifting 90 percent of your RM right off the bat, studies have shown that beginners can experience gains in strength using as little as 45 percent of their one-rep maximum for a particular exercise.

Different phases of a periodized weight-training program will feature different levels of intensity. The Strength and Power phases will normally feature more weight with fewer repetitions, say, six or fewer. In contrast, the Hypertrophy phase will feature lower weight and more repetitions, such as eight to 12 or more on some exercises.

You can adjust the intensity yourself during a program, if you feel you can add weight safely. The key is to make sure you can do at least two extra repetitions at a particular weight before adding weight, or four or more extra repetitions on the last set of the heavy days of the program. You should not add more than five pounds a week during the first few weeks. Be sure to resist the urge to add too much weight too soon, as soreness or injury could result.

Athletes in different sports have different requirements for training intensity. Athletes in sports that require agility and explosive movements will probably want to use heavier loads with low repetitions, while athletes in endurance sports may be more interested in lighter loads with higher repetitions, which can also have the beneficial effect of preventing injury through joint strengthening.

Finally, if you are a competitive athlete, the time of year can also dictate your training intensity. Not surprisingly, you may want to train more intensely during the off-season, and gradually taper your training as the preseason approaches. During in-season competition, training can take place on a less intense level that will maintain strength without placing too much stress on the body.

Number of Sets

It is generally agreed that you need to perform at least three sets of an exercise to make gains in muscle strength and size. There are many exceptions, of course. One exception is beginners, who will probably do one or two sets for the first few weeks of a preparatory program. Another is in-season athletes, who sometimes do one set of several exercises to help maintain the muscle gains they made during the off-season.

Type of Exercises

This will depend partly on what sport you play and what specific muscles you want to train, keeping in mind that a balance must be maintained so that no areas are neglected. You may also have the choice of using free weights or a weight machine such as a Universal or Nautilus. Free weights more closely resemble natural motions, but are more difficult to control and thus require more work on technique. Weight machines are easier to use but offer less range of motion.

You also have your choice of single-joint exercises, such as wrist curls or leg extensions, and multijoint exercises, such as squats or dead lifts. As the name implies, multijoint exercises place stress on more than one muscle, so you may end up having to do fewer exercises during your workout. The downside is that not all the muscles will get the same benefit. In single-joint exercises, you are isolating a specific muscle group but may have to do more exercises during your workout to cover all the bases.

Order of Exercises

The order of exercises in any workout should never be random. The aim is to overload your muscles enough so that you get the most benefit from each exercise without putting too much strain on any individual muscle groups.

For beginners, it is usually best to use a basic order of exercises that alternate muscle groups. For instance, in the General Preparatory program described in this book, one workout features leg extensions followed by leg curls—working first the thigh muscles and then the hamstrings—then twisting sit-ups followed by hip abduction and adduction; then standing calf exercises followed by back extensions.

Exercise order is also determined by the training cycle. In the Hypertrophy phase, the emphasis is on alternating muscle groups, while the Strength and Power phases both feature more difficult, multijoint exercises such as squats and lunges. These are performed at the beginning of the workout, when you are fresh and more able to concentrate on technique. In general, the more difficult exercises should be performed first. If your muscles are fatigued before you attempt these exercises, you may not get the maximum benefit of the exercise.

The sport-specific phase of your program will feature multijoint exercises that are geared toward the requirements of your specific sport, and you will usually perform these at the beginning of the workout.

Rest Periods During and Between Workouts

Like exercise order, the length of rest periods can have a big effect on what you get out of your workout. You will notice in the sample training programs described in this book that the length of rest periods is not always the same from one week to the next, and that as you progress through a program you will be asked to shorten the rest periods between sets of exercises. This has to be done gradually, to prevent nausea that can result from the buildup of lactic acid in your muscles.

The amount of rest you need between sets is determined by your physical condition, how far along you are in the specific program, what types of exercises you are performing, and the level of intensity at which you are performing them. For instance, high-intensity exercises that are performed for approximately 30 seconds can require up to three minutes for your body to replenish the phosphagen stores in your muscles. If your goal is to train for maximum strength and you are lifting weights at or near your repetition maximum (RM), you may need more than three minutes between sets. If your goal is to achieve hypertrophy (increase in muscle size) or muscle endurance and you are performing more repetitions at lower weights, you may need fewer than one to two minutes of rest between sets. This roughly works out to a 1:1 ratio, since 10–12 repetitions of an exercise done correctly will take about one minute. Athletes who need to sustain maximum energy over a few minutes, such as middle-distance runners, sprint swimmers, and wrestlers, can benefit from this type of format, as it gets their muscles used to the high lactic acid buildup that results from those activities.

Since everyone is different, you may benefit from longer rest periods between sets. This is especially true for heavier athletes, and for those athletes who are just beginning a weight training program. In some cases, coaches and athletes check for the heart rate to return to a certain level before beginning the next set. Consult your coach or trainer if you are unsure about how much rest to take between sets at any point during your program.

Rest periods between workouts are at least as important. As discussed elsewhere in this book, your muscles usually need a minimum of 24 hours to recover from a workout and adapt to the increased stress. For this reason, the programs contained in this book are based on a maximum of three workouts per week, with fewer workouts (and more rest time) during the early weeks of the beginning phase of the programs. Other programs can feature as many as six training days during a week, but these are specialized programs that focus on different muscle groups each day.

PERIODIZATION PHASES

Periodized training is training that is divided into different phases and cycles, with the overall goal of getting you in peak condition for the beginning of a season or the onset of a major competition or tournament. Accordingly, there are several terms that describe these different aspects of your program.

Your overall training program is called a **macrocycle,** and describes the full training year, usually beginning and ending with the conclusion of a season. Within each macrocycle are **mesocycles,** which are the various phases that make up a periodized program and are described in the next section: Functional Strength Base, Preparatory, Hypertrophy, Strength and Power. Within each mesocycle are **microcycles,** which are defined as one week of training.

6

SAMPLE PREPARATORY PROGRAM

This section describes a 25-week periodized weight-training program for beginners. If the competition season occurs during any program, cut back on volume of exercises by decreasing the number of sets and reps. Also, you should train one or two times per week in-season instead of three, and train no closer than two days before a competition.

The phases are defined as follows:

FUNCTIONAL STRENGTH BASE
Length: 5 weeks
Goals: Perform body resistance exercises like push-ups, sit-ups, pull-ups, etc., to prepare muscles for the next phase, when weight training will begin. Practice techniques of resistance exercises (squats, for instance) to prepare for next phase.

PREPARATORY
Length: 7 weeks
Goals: Prepare your muscles and joints for overloading in the next phase by doing multiple-joint resistance exercises with minimal overload. Pinpoint individual muscle groups and strengthen not only the muscle but the ligaments and the bones. Basic preparation readies your body to take on overload resistance.

HYPERTROPHY/STRENGTH
Length: 7 weeks
Goals: Increase muscle mass and size (hypertrophy), which will serve as a base for the following phase, Strength and Power. This is accomplished by using relatively low resistance but high numbers of

repetitions. Introduce new exercises (Romanian dead lift, standing row, lunge, and so on). Rest periods are short to moderate, so that your muscles do not completely recover before you start the next set.

STRENGTH/POWER
Length: 5 weeks
Goals: Increase muscle strength by using more resistance but fewer repetitions (include a full recovery period between sets). Introduce explosive exercises and reduce the total number of exercises performed.

ACTIVE REST
Length: 1 week
Goals: Take a week off from weight training and pursue other sports activities. Can be taken during the middle of one of the phases, especially during a holiday week. Return gradually to program by using less weight or doing one fewer set during first week back. These active rest weeks can be scheduled and taken around holidays and vacations. They can also be taken if you feel that you are overtraining.

FUNCTIONAL STRENGTH BASE PROGRAM

Before beginning any weight-training program, it is important to begin with functional training, which aims to develop basic strength of the muscles, bones, tendons, and ligaments and prepare you for the preparatory phase. It will also help you improve your posture and balance and help prevent injuries. Instead of weights, you will be mostly using your own body weight as resistance.

As with any training program, make sure you have been medically cleared for this type of training, and do the following exercises only under the supervision of a qualified, certified adult coach who can teach the proper techniques that will help avoid injury and achieve positive results.

The Functional Strength Base program should be performed two days a week for five weeks.

WEEKS 1 & 2
DAY 1

Warm up Jump rope: moderate pace for 3 minutes (use different steps if possible)
Stretching Hamstrings, quadriceps, groin, leg swings, shoulder swings

Exercises	Sets	Reps
Practice overhead squats with wooden dowel	2	15
Bent knee sit-ups	2	20
Wall push-ups	2	20
Upper back pull-ups from squat rack	2	10
Practice bench press with wooden dowel	2	25
Medicine ball trunk twist	2	15 (each side)

DAY 2

Warm up   Jumping jacks (35 reps)
Stretching   Hamstrings, quadriceps, groin, leg swings, shoulder swings

Exercises	Sets	Reps
Practice hang clean with wooden dowel	2	15
Practice dead lift with hex bar (no weight)	2	15
Walking lunge (front & back)	2	15
Crunches	2	20
Push-ups	2	10
Medicine ball sumo swing to eye height	2	15

WEEK 3

Increase sets to 3 and repetitions by 5 for each exercise from Week 1. For warmup, jump rope for five minutes and do jumping jacks for 50 repetitions.

WEEK 4

DAY 1

Warm up   Jump rope: moderate pace for 5 minutes (use different steps if possible)
Stretching   Hamstrings, quadriceps, groin, leg swings, shoulder swings

Exercises	Sets	Reps
Practice overhead squats with wooden dowel	3	25
Pull-ups (modified if needed)	3	10
Squat thrusts	2	20
Twisting sit-ups (feet on ground)	3	25
Dips (modified if needed)	2	10
Practice bench press with wooden dowel	2	25
Seated medicine ball side twist (throw to wall)	2	15 (each side)

DAY 2

Warm up   Jumping jacks (50 reps)
Stretching   Hamstrings, quadriceps, groin, leg swings, shoulder swings

DAY 2 *(continued)*

Exercises	Sets	Reps
Practice hang clean with wooden dowel	2	20
Practice dead lift with hex bar (no weight)	2	25
Squat thrust	2	15
Crunches	3	20
Walking lunge (front & side)	2	20
Push-ups	3	18
Medicine ball sumo swing to overhead & toe raise	2	25

WEEK 5

Increase repetitions by 5 for each exercise from Week 4. If this is too difficult, do whatever number is possible while maintaining good form.

PREPARATORY PROGRAM

The preparatory phase is designed to prepare your muscles beyond the Functional Strength Base Program described earlier. What you are doing is actually preparing your body to work the various muscle groups. You do this by performing multiple-joint exercises—exercises that put stress on more than one joint—that will also pinpoint specific muscle groups and strengthen not only those muscles but the surrounding ligaments and the bones.

You will experience minimal overload during this phase and gradually move toward increasing the overload in the next phase, Hypertrophy. You will also learn proper lifting technique for several exercises.

Follow this procedure for the supplemental exercises, remembering to increase the reps by two before you increase the weight.

The preparatory program should be performed three days a week for five weeks.

MONDAY

Exercises	Sets	Reps
Front squats	2	10
Bench press	2	10
Lat pulls	2	12
Crunches	2	20
Shoulder press	2	12
Triceps extensions	2	12
Biceps curls	2	12
Back extensions	2	12

WEDNESDAY

	Sets	Reps
Hang clean	2	5
Dead lift (done with hex bar)	2	5
Leg extensions	2	12
Leg curls (hamstrings)	2	12
Twisting sit-ups	2	20
Hip abduction/adduction	2	12
Standing calf	2	12
Back extension	2	12

FRIDAY

	Sets	Reps
Squat	2	10
90-degree bench press	2	10
Low row	2	12
Leg curls (hamstrings)	2	12
Seated medicine ball side twist	2	20
Biceps curls	2	12
Tricep extension	2	12

HYPERTROPHY/STRENGTH PROGRAM

In this phase you will be making several adjustments from the preparatory phase, and you will also be learning several new exercises. For some of the exercises that use weights, you will do more sets but fewer repetitions, but still increase the amount of weight once you can do two extra reps at a particular weight. You should try to gradually increase the number of reps for the exercises that use only your body weight (crunches, twisting sit-ups).

For the new exercises—incline bench press, lunge, standing row, good morning exercise, Romanian dead lift, and side lunge—start by doing lifts with the 45-pound bar (or 15-pound aluminum bar if the 45-pound bar is too heavy for good technique) until you can complete the required number of sets with proper technique. If you are beginning with two sets of 10 repetitions, increase the weight by five pounds in the second week when you can do two extra repetitions at the original weight. Do two sets of 10 reps at the new weight, and do not increase the weight by more than five pounds per week. Always increase the reps first, then the weight. As a guide, you can increase by 10 percent on lower body large muscle groups, 5 percent on upper body multi-joint exercises like bench press, and 2.5 percent for single-joint upper body exercises like bicep curls.

The Hypertrophy/Strength program should be performed three days a week for seven weeks.

MONDAY

	Sets	Reps
Front squats	3	8
Incline bench press	2	10
Pull-ups	2	12
Crunches	2	20
Standing row	2	10
Dips	2	12
Preacher curls	2	10
Good morning exercise	2	10

WEDNESDAY

	Sets	Reps
Hang clean	3	5
Dead lift with hex bar	2	5
Leg extensions	2	10
Romanian dead lift	2	10
Twisting sit-ups	2	20
Side lunge	2	10
Standing calf	2	10

FRIDAY

	Sets	Reps
Lunge	2	10
Bench press	3	8
Leg extension	2	10
Low row	2	10
Leg curls (hamstrings)	2	10
Seated medicine ball side twist	2	20
Biceps curls	2	10
Tricep extension	2	10

STRENGTH/POWER PROGRAM

Several key adjustments highlight the Strength/Power phase. This program will improve strength as well as explosiveness. Repetitions will be lower than in the previous phase, and more explosive exercises will be introduced. More sets will be added to many of the exercises, while the number of exercises will be reduced. As in previous phases, when two extra reps of an exercise can be performed, increase the weight by five pounds. For exercises involving body weight, sets and reps will increase.

For the new exercises—high pull and step ups—make sure to start with the 45-pound bar and concentrate on technique before adding any weight. When you are comfortable at a weight, do two sets of 10 reps. When you can do two sets of 12 reps comfortably, increase the weight by five pounds. Do not increase by more than five pounds per week. Do two sets of 10 reps again at the new weight (or five or eight, depending on how the exercise is listed in the program).

The Strength/Power program should be performed three days a week for five weeks.

MONDAY

	Sets	Reps
Front squats	3	6
Bench press	2	6
Crunches	3	25
High pull	2	10
Romanian dead lift	2	10

WEDNESDAY

	Sets	Reps
Hang clean	3	5
Dead lift with hex bar	3	5
Step ups	2	8
Twisting sit-ups	3	25
Lat pulls	3	8

FRIDAY

	Sets	Reps
Squat	2	6
Bench press	3	6
Low row	3	10
Leg curls (hamstrings)	3	10
Seated medicine ball side twist	2	20

7

SPORT-SPECIFIC PROGRAMS

After completing the general Functional Strength, Preparatory, Hypertrophy/Strength, and Strength/Power programs, you should be ready to start focusing on a weight training program that addresses the needs of specific sports. While each program features some exercises that simulate different movements required in each sport, there are many similarities between the programs.

Take particular notice of the training variables that will change during the different weeks of each program:

- Transition week: During the first week you will perform two sets of each exercise to prepare your muscles and joints gradually for subsequent phases.
- Volume: The amount of weight you lift will range from 85 and 100 percent of your repetition maximum (RM).
- Sets: During the middle weeks of the program, you will do some exercises for four sets instead of three.
- Rest periods: These range from one minute for single-joint exercises early in the Hypertrophy phase to four minutes for complex exercises during the Power phase.
- Exercise order: During some weeks you will do the same exercises on the same days, but the order will change to break up the routine a little and provide your muscles with different types of overload.
- General intensity: This will range from light to medium to heavy, with the light days occurring during the early weeks. With a few exceptions, you will have a maximum of one heavy training day per week.

With all programs, it is absolutely essential to start out gradually when you are learning a new exercise. Particularly in the Power phases, when you will be performing complex exercises that require attention to technique, it pays to practice the exercise with a light weight—or, in some cases, a wooden dowel—until you have mastered the motion and are able to progress to more weight. Always learn new exercises under the supervision of a trainer or coach.

Once you have mastered a particular exercise and performed it with weights, you may find yourself wanting to add more weight to get more benefit out of the exercise. This is the correct thing to do, as you can only increase your strength and power by continuously overloading your muscles. As a general rule, make sure you can do at least four more repetitions in your final set at the current weight before you increase the RM for your next workout. Never increase the weight by more than five pounds per week, and make sure to go back to the original number of repetitions at the higher weight. As a general rule, increase 10 percent for lower body and multijoint exercises like squats, 5 percent for upper body exercises, and 2.5 percent for arms.

AGILITY DRILLS

Another training tool that is as important to athletes as strength and power is agility. Having well-developed muscles will not mean much if you lack the coordination to put them into action. The goal of doing agility drills is to develop quickness, foot speed, coordination, and balance, and improve the ability to change direction rapidly and under control. No conditioning program can be complete without these drills. They can be performed as a precursor to your weight-training workout, as well as on days when you are not lifting.

There are an almost infinite number of agility drills to choose from, and some are listed in the following chapters in the programs tailored to specific sports, such as the dot drill and form running. Other agility drills focus on lateral movement, stopping and starting, pivoting, and changing direction quickly. Your coach or trainer will know which types of agility drills apply to your sport, and he or she will be able to demonstrate the proper techniques.

PROGRAM PHASES

Transition Week

The Transition week serves to prepare your joints and muscles for the stresses they will absorb during the Hypertrophy program. Each workout begins with nonresistance agility drills, which are described in the Exercises section. All exercises are performed for two sets, with three minutes of rest time between each set. For new exercises, use a wooden dowel or a light weight to practice technique before adding weight, and always practice under the supervision of a trainer or coach.

Hypertrophy Phase

The eight-week Hypertrophy program follows a progression from moderate intensity to heavy, and back to moderate. Note that the length of rest periods begins to decrease in Week 3, and additional sets are added beginning in Week 4. Weeks 5 through 7 are the most intense, followed by a scaling back of intensity in Week 8.

Strength Phase

The intensity picks up more quickly in the Strength program than in the Hypertrophy program, as you begin performing four sets of all exercises in Week 2. Week 3 features back-to-back heavy intensity days, so make sure you are well rested and properly warmed up before you begin. In Week 4 you will use your 100 percent RM for the first time on Day 3, and the number of repetitions for many of the exercises will decrease by set as noted below.

Week 5 is in some ways the opposite of Week 4, as you start with a heavy intensity workout and then taper off to medium intensity days. Week 6 starts with a light workout day and progresses to heavy intensity on Day 3. The amount of weight is slightly decreased from Week 5, as are the number of repetitions.

Where exercises are listed with a plus sign, try to do extra repetitions on your final set. If you can increase the repetitions on your final set by four, increase your RM for the exercise by no more than five pounds for your next workout.

Power Phase

The six-week Power program differs significantly from the Hypertrophy and Strength programs. You will perform fewer exercises, mostly at lower repetitions, and, more important, you will perform complex exercises to develop strength and explosiveness. These exercises involve more than one movement and combine resistance with plyometric motions, such as back squats combined with squat jumps. Do the weight exercise first, and immediately follow with the plyometric exercise. You will need a four-minute rest period between sets for these exercises. It is especially important to learn these complex exercises under the supervision of a trained instructor, and to practice them until you have the technique mastered before attempting them at full intensity.

Complex Exercises

Complex exercises, which combine a weight exercise and a nonweight plyometric exercise, are found in the Power program and are listed in boldface type. Do all repetitions of the weight exercise first, then follow immediately with the nonweight exercise. Make sure to take a four-minute break between each set. The descriptions for all individual exercises are found in chapter 13.

8

SPORT-SPECIFIC PROGRAMS: BASKETBALL

Basketball requires repeated explosive movements that involve coordination of your upper and lower body. Imagine yourself jumping to grab a rebound: you use your calves, hamstrings, quadriceps (thigh muscles), back, and hips to get off the ground, and then your chest muscles, shoulders, biceps, and back muscles to grab the ball away from an opposing player. Then, you use the same lower-body joints and muscles to absorb the shock when you land.

The basketball program described in this section features several exercises that are designed to simulate specific body movements that occur during a game, as well as general functional exercises aimed at strengthening your muscles and joints.

For example, incline presses are basically bench presses performed at an angle with your arms in front of you, similar to the position you are in when you are reaching for the ball or grabbing a rebound. Dead lifts, power shrugs (high pulls) strengthen your shoulders and hips and help your muscles work together when you jump off the floor. Medicine ball exercises strengthen your trunk and shoulders and simulate the type of twisting motions you make repeatedly during a game.

In addition, one-leg squats to a toe raise mimic the motion you make when you are shooting a layup. Similarly, side lunges prepare you for the lateral motion, or shuffling, that you have to do when you play defense.

(Note: where triceps is listed, check with your coach or trainer for which of three exercises to do: close grip bench press, extension, or French curl).

BASKETBALL PROGRAM

New exercises

High pull

Shoulder raises with dumbbell

Push press

Pec fly

Standing rows

Medicine ball seated twist

Power shrug

Incline press

Additional equipment

Medicine ball

TRANSITION WEEK

DAY 1 (MEDIUM)

Rest Period: 3 minutes
Repetition Maximum (RM): 85%

	Sets	Reps
High pull	2	6
Front squats	2	10
Bench press	2	10
Leg curls (hamstrings)	2	10
Lat pulls (close grip)	2	10
Twisting sit-ups	2	20
Shoulder raises with dumbbell	2	12
Crunches	2	20
Biceps curls	2	12
Standing calf	2	12
Triceps	2	12

DAY 2 (MEDIUM)

Rest Period: 3 minutes
Repetition Maximum (RM): 85%

	Sets	Reps
Push press	2	10
Dead lift with hex bar	2	5
Pec fly	2	10

DAY 2 (MEDIUM) (continued)

	Sets	Reps
Seated leg curl	2	10
Low row	2	10
Seated calf	2	12
Standing row	2	12
Medicine ball seated twist	2	20
Triceps	2	12
Hip abduction/adduction	2	12
Wrist curls	2	12

DAY 3 (MEDIUM)

Rest Period: 3 minutes
Repetition Maximum (RM): 85%

	Sets	Reps
Power shrug	2	10
Incline press	2	10
Lat pulls (wide grip)	2	10
Hip abduction/adduction	2	10
Pullover	2	12
Leg extension	2	12
Twisting sit-ups	2	20
Biceps curls	2	12
Crunches	2	20
Wrist curls	2	12

HYPERTROPHY PROGRAM—8 WEEKS

WEEK 1

DAY 1 (MEDIUM)

Rest Period: 3 minutes
Repetition Maximum (RM): 90%

	Sets	Reps
High pull	3	6
Front squats	3	10
Bench press	3	10
Leg curls (hamstrings)	3	10
Lat pulls (close grip)	3	10
Twisting sit-ups	3	20
Shoulder raises with dumbbell	3	12
Crunches	3	20
Biceps curls	3	12

	Sets	Reps
Standing calf	3	12
Triceps	3	12

DAY 2 (MEDIUM)

Rest Period: 3 minutes
Repetition Maximum (RM): 90%

	Sets	Reps
Push press	3	10
Dead lift with hex bar	3	5
Pec fly	3	10
Seated leg curl	3	10
Low row	3	10
Seated calf	3	12
Standing row	3	12
Medicine ball seated twist	3	20
Triceps	3	12
Hip abduction/adduction	3	12
Wrist curls	3	12

DAY 3 (MEDIUM)

Rest Period: 3 minutes
Repetition Maximum (RM): 90%

	Sets	Reps
Power shrug	3	10
Incline press	3	10
Lat pulls (wide grip)	3	10
Hip abduction/adduction	3	10
Pullover	3	12
Leg extension	3	12
Twisting sit-ups	3	20
Biceps curls	3	12
Crunches	3	20
Wrist curls	3	12

WEEK 2

DAY 1 (HEAVY)

Rest Period: 3 minutes
Repetition Maximum (RM): 95%

	Sets	Reps
High pull	3	6
Front squats	3	10

DAY 1 (HEAVY) (continued)

	Sets	Reps
Bench press	3	10
Leg curls (hamstrings)	3	10
Lat pulls (close grip)	3	10
Twisting sit-ups	3	20
Standing row	3	12
Crunches	3	20
Biceps curls	3	12
Standing calf	3	12

DAY 2 (LIGHT)

Rest Period: 3 minutes
Repetition Maximum (RM): 85%

	Sets	Reps
Push press	3	10
Dead lift with hex bar	3	5
Pec fly	3	10
Seated leg curl	3	10
Low row	3	10
Seated calf	3	12
Shoulder raise with dumbbell	3	12
Medicine ball seated twist	3	20
Triceps	3	12
Hip abduction/adduction	3	12
Wrist curls	3	12

DAY 3 (MEDIUM)

Rest Period: 3 minutes
Repetition Maximum (RM): 90%

	Sets	Reps
Power shrug	3	10
Incline press	3	10
Lat pulls (wide grip)	3	10
Hip abduction/adduction	3	10
Pullover	3	12
Leg extension	3	12
Twisting sit-ups	3	20
Biceps curls	3	12
Crunches	3	20
Wrist curls	3	12

WEEK 3
DAY 1 (LIGHT)

Rest Period: variable
Repetition Maximum(RM): 85%

	Sets	Reps	Rest Period
High pull	3	6	3 minutes
Back squats	3	10	3 minutes
Bench press	3	10	3 minutes
Leg curls (hamstrings)	3	10	3 minutes
Lat pulls (close grip)	3	10	3 minutes
Twisting sit-ups	3	20	2 minutes
Standing row	3	12	2 minutes
Crunches	3	20	2 minutes
Biceps curls	3	12	2 minutes
Standing calf	3	12	2 minutes
Triceps	3	12	2 minutes

DAY 2 (HEAVY)

Rest Period: variable
Repetition Maximum (RM): 100%

	Sets	Reps	Rest Period
Push press	3	10+	3 minutes
Dead lift with hex bar	3	5+	3 minutes
Pec fly	3	10+	3 minutes
Seated leg curl	3	10+	3 minutes
Low row	3	10+	3 minutes
Seated calf	3	12+	2 minutes
Shoulder raise with dumbbell	3	12+	2 minutes
Medicine ball seated twist	3	20+	2 minutes
Triceps	3	12+	2 minutes
Hip abduction/adduction	3	12+	2 minutes
Wrist curls	3	12+	2 minutes

DAY 3 (MEDIUM)

Rest Period: variable
Repetition Maximum (RM): 95%

	Sets	Reps	Rest Period
Power shrug	3	10	3 minutes
Incline press	3	10	3 minutes
Lat pulls (wide grip)	3	10	3 minutes
Hip abduction/adduction	3	10	2 minutes
Pullover	3	12	2 minutes
Leg extension	3	12	2 minutes

DAY 3 (MEDIUM) (continued)

	Sets	Reps	Rest Period
Twisting sit-ups	3	20	2 minutes
Biceps curls	3	12	2 minutes
Crunches	3	20	2 minutes
Wrist curls	3	12	2 minutes

WEEK 4
DAY 1 (HEAVY)

Rest Period: 2 minutes (3 minutes for high pull)
Repetition Maximum (RM): variable

	Sets	Reps	Rest Period	RM
High pull	4	6+	3 minutes	85%-90%-95%-100%
Front squats	4	10+	2 minutes	85%-90%-95%-100%
Bench press	4	10+	2 minutes	85%-90%-95%-100%
Leg curls (hamstrings)	3	10+	2 minutes	85%
Lat pulls (close grip)	3	20+	2 minutes	100%
Twisting sit-ups	3	20+	2 minutes	
Standing row	3	10+	2 minutes	100%
Crunches	3	20+	2 minutes	
Biceps curls	3	10+	2 minutes	100%
Standing calf	3	10+	2 minutes	100%
Triceps	3	10+	2 minutes	100%

DAY 2 (MEDIUM)

Rest Period: 2 minutes (3 minutes for push press)
Repetition Maximum (RM): 90%

	Sets	Reps	Rest Period	RM
Push press	4	10	3 minutes	90%
Dead lift with hex bar	4	5	3 minutes	90%
Pec fly	3	10	2 minutes	90%
Seated leg curl	3	10	2 minutes	90%
Low row	3	10	2 minutes	90%
Seated calf	3	10	2 minutes	90%
Shoulder raise with dumbbell	3	10	2 minutes	90%
Medicine ball seated twist	3	20	2 minutes	
Triceps	3	10	2 minutes	90%
Hip abduction/ adduction	3	10	2 minutes	90%
Wrist curls	3	10	2 minutes	

DAY 3 (LIGHT)

Rest Period: 2 minutes (3 minutes for power shrug)
Repetition Maximum (RM): 85%

	Sets	Reps	Rest Period	RM
Power shrug	4	10	3 minutes	85%
Incline press	4	10	2 minutes	85%
Lat pulls (wide grip)	4	10	2 minutes	85%
Hip abduction/ adduction	3	10	2 minutes	85%
Pullover	3	12	2 minutes	85%
Leg extension	3	12	2 minutes	85%
Twisting sit-ups	3	20	2 minutes	
Biceps curls	3	12	2 minutes	85%
Crunches	3	20	2 minutes	
Wrist curls	3	12	2 minutes	

WEEK 5

For the final set of the high pull on Day 1, do 10 repetitions using the 45-pound bar.

DAY 1 (MEDIUM)

Rest Period: variable
Repetition Maximum (RM): 90%

	Sets	Reps	Rest Period	RM
High pull	4	6/10	3 minutes	90%-90%-90%-45 lbs.
Back squats	4	10	2 minutes	90%
Bench press	4	10	2 minutes	90%
Leg curls (hamstrings)	3	10	1 minute	90%
Lat pulls (close grip)	3	10	2 minutes	90%
Twisting sit-ups	3	20	1 minute	
Standing row	3	10	2 minutes	90%
Crunches	3	20	1 minute	
Biceps curls	3	10	1 minute	90%
Standing calf	3	10	1 minute	90%
Triceps	3	10	1 minute	90%

DAY 2 (MEDIUM)

Rest Period: variable
Repetition Maximum (RM): 90%

	Sets	Reps	Rest Period	RM
Push press	4	10	3 minutes	90%
Dead lift with hex bar	3	10	3 minutes	90%

DAY 2 (MEDIUM) (continued)

	Sets	Reps	Rest Period	RM
Pec fly	3	10	2 minutes	90%
Seated leg curl	3	10	2 minutes	90%
Low row	3	10	2 minutes	90%
Seated calf	3	10	1 minute	90%
Shoulder raise with dumbbell	3	10	1 minute	90%
Medicine ball seated twist	3	20	1 minute	
Triceps	3	10	1 minute	90%
Hip abduction/ adduction	3	10	1 minute	90%
Wrist curls	3	10	1 minute	

DAY 3 (HEAVY)

Rest Period: variable
Repetition Maximum (RM): variable

	Sets	Reps	Rest Period	RM
Power shrug	4	10+	3 minutes	100%
Incline press	4	10+	2 minutes	85%-90%-95%-100%
Lat pulls (wide grip)	4	10+	2 minutes	85%-90%-95%-100%
Hip abduction/ adduction	3	10+	1 minute	100%
Pullover	3	10+	1 minute	100%
Leg extension	3	10+	1 minute	100%
Twisting sit-ups	3	20+	1 minute	
Biceps curls	3	10+	1 minute	100%
Crunches	3	20+	1 minute	
Wrist curls	3	10+	1 minute	100%

WEEK 6

DAY 1 (MEDIUM)

Rest Period: 1 minute (3 minutes for high pull)
Repetition Maximum (RM): 90%

	Sets	Reps	Rest Period	RM
High pull	4	6/10	3 minutes	90%-90%-90%-45 lbs.
Back squats	4	10	1 minute	90%
Bench press with dumbbell	4	10	1 minute	90%
Lat pulls (close grip)	3	10	1 minute	90%

	Sets	Reps	Rest Period	RM
Leg curls (hamstrings)	3	10	1 minute	90%
Standing calf	3	10	1 minute	90%
Twisting sit-ups	3	20	1 minute	
Standing row	3	10	1 minute	90%
Crunches	3	20	1 minute	
Biceps curls	3	10	1 minute	90%
Triceps	3	10	1 minute	90%

DAY 2 (HEAVY)

Rest Period: variable
Repetition Maximum (RM): variable

	Sets	Reps	Rest Period	RM
Push press	4	10+	3 minutes	100%
Dead lift with hex bar	4	5+	3 minutes	85%-90%-95%-100% 100%
Pec fly	3	10+	1 minute	100%
Seated leg curl	3	10+	1 minute	100%
Low row	4	10+	2 minutes	85%-90%-95%-100%
Seated calf	3	10+	1 minute	100%
Shoulder raise with dumbbell	3	10+	1 minute	100%
Medicine ball seated twist	3	20+	1 minute	
Triceps	3	10+	1 minute	100%
Hip abduction/ adduction	3	10+	1 minute	100%
Wrist curls	3	10+	1 minute	100%

DAY 3 (MEDIUM)

Rest Period: 1 minute (3 minutes for power shrug)
Repetition Maximum (RM): 90%

	Sets	Reps	Rest Period
Power shrug	4	10	3 minutes
Incline press	4	10	1 minute
Lat pulls (wide grip)	4	10	1 minute
Hip abduction/ adduction	3	10	1 minute
Pullover	3	10	1 minute
Leg extension	3	10	1 minute
Twisting sit-ups	3	20	1 minute
Biceps curls	3	10	1 minute
Crunches	3	20	1 minute
Wrist curls	3	10	1 minute

WEEK 7
DAY 1 (HEAVY)

Rest Period: variable
Repetition Maximum (RM): variable

	Sets	Reps	Rest Period	RM
High pull	4	6	3 minutes	85%-90%-95%-100%
Leg press	4	10	2 minutes	85%-90%-95%-100%
Bench press with dumbbell	4	10	2 minutes	85%-90%-95%-100%
Leg curls (hamstrings)	4	10	1 minute	100%
Standing calf	3	10	1 minute	100%
Twisting sit-ups	3	20/10	1 minute	100%
Standing row	3	10	1 minute	100%
Crunches	3	10	1 minute	100%
Back extension	3	20	1 minute	100%
Triceps	3	10	1 minute	100%

DAY 2 (MEDIUM)

Rest Period: 1 minute (3 minutes for push press)
Repetition Maximum (RM): 90%

	Sets	Reps	Rest Period
Push press	4	10	3 minutes
Lunge	4	10	1 minute
Pec fly	4	10	1 minute
Low row	4	10	1 minute
Shoulder raise with dumbbell	3	10	1 minute
Seated leg curl	3	10	1 minute
Hip abduction/ adduction	3	10	1 minute
Seated calf	3	10	1 minute
Medicine ball seated twist	3	20	1 minute
Wrist curls	3	10	1 minute

DAY 3 (HEAVY)

Rest Period: variable
Repetition Maximum (RM): variable

	Sets	Reps	Rest Period	RM
Power shrug	4	10+	3 minutes	100%
Incline press	4	10+	2 minutes	85%-90%-95%-100%

	Sets	Reps	Rest Period	RM
Lat pulls (wide grip) adduction	4	10+	2 minutes	85%-90%-95%-100%
Pullover	3	10+	1 minute	100%
Hip abduction/ adduction	4	10/12+	1 minute	85%-90%-95%-100%
Leg extension	3	10+	1 minute	100%
Twisting sit-ups	3	20+	1 minute	
Biceps curls	3	10+	1 minute	100%
Crunches	3	20+	1 minute	
Good morning	3	10+	1 minute	100%

WEEK 8

DAY 1 (MEDIUM)

Rest Period: 1 minute (3 minutes for high pull)
Repetition Maximum (RM): 90%

	Sets	Reps	Rest Period	RM
High pull	3	6	3 minutes	90%
Leg press	3	10	1 minute	90%
Bench press with dumbbell	3	10	1 minute	90%
Leg curls (hamstrings)	3	10	1 minute	90%
Standing calf	3	10	1 minute	90%
Twisting sit-ups	3	20	1 minute	90%
Standing row	3	10	1 minute	90%
Crunches	3	10	1 minute	
Back extension	3	20	1 minute	90%
Triceps	3	10	1 minute	90%

DAY 2 (MEDIUM)

Rest Period: 1 minute (3 minutes for push press)
Repetition Maximum (RM): 90%

	Sets	Reps	Rest Period
Push press	3	10	3 minutes
Lunge	3	10	1 minute
Pec fly	3	10	1 minute
Low row	3	10	1 minute
Should raise with dumbbell	3	10	1 minute
Seated leg curl	3	10	1 minute
Hip abduction/ adduction	3	10	1 minute
Seated calf	3	10	1 minute

DAY 2 (MEDIUM) (continued)

	Sets	Reps	Rest Period
Medicine ball seated twist	3	20	1 minute
Wrist curls	3	10	1 minute

DAY 3 (MEDIUM)

Rest Period: variable
Repetition Maximum (RM): 85%

	Sets	Reps	Rest Period
Power shrug	3	10	3 minutes
Incline press	3	10	2 minutes
Lat pulls (wide grip)	3	10	2 minutes
Pullover	3	10	1 minute
Hip abduction/adduction	3	10	1 minute
Leg extension	3	10	1 minute
Twisting sit-ups	3	20	1 minute
Biceps curls	3	10	1 minute
Crunches	3	20	1 minute
Good morning	3	10	1 minute

STRENGTH PROGRAM—6 WEEKS

New exercises

Hang clean

Back squat

Medicine ball sit-up and twist

Balance ball low abs

Medicine ball lunge with twist to front leg

Step-ups

Additional equipment

Medicine ball

Parallel bars

Balance ball

Step-up box

WEEK 1

DAY 1 (MEDIUM)

Rest Period: 3 minutes (1 minute for practice hang clean)
Repetition Maximum (RM): 90%

	Sets	Reps
Practice hang clean (using wooden dowel)	3	10
Back squats	3	8
Incline press with dumbbell	3	8
Romanian dead lift	3	8
Leg curl (hamstrings)	3	8
Single rows with dumbbell	3	8
Side lunge	3	8
Twisting sit-ups	3	25+
Standing calf	3	8
Crunches	3	25

DAY 2 (MEDIUM)

Rest Period: 3 minutes
Repetition Maximum (RM): 90%

	Sets	Reps
Push press	3	6
Dead lift with hex bar	3	6
Medicine ball sit-up and twist	3	20+
Pull-ups (modified if needed)	3	8
Balance ball low abs	3	10+
Low row	3	8
Shoulder raises with dumbbell	3	10
Dips (negative if needed)	3	8
Biceps curls	3	10
Wrist curls	3	10

DAY 3 (MEDIUM)

Rest Period: 3 minutes
Repetition Maximum (RM): 90%

	Sets	Reps
High pull	3	6
Bench press	3	10
Medicine ball lunge with twist to front leg	3	10
Twisting sit-ups	3	25+
Balance ball hamstrings	3	10
Step-ups	3	10
Plyometric sit-ups (low abs)	3	10+
Pullover	3	10
Rotator cuff	3	15

WEEK 2
DAY 1 (MEDIUM)
Rest Period: 3 minutes (1 minute for practice hang clean)
Repetition Maximum (RM): 90%

	Sets	Reps
Practice hang clean (using wooden dowel)	3	10
Back squats	3	8
Incline press with dumbbell	3	8
Romanian dead lift	3	8
Leg curl (hamstrings)	3	8
Single rows with dumbbell	3	8
Side lunge	3	8
Twisting sit-ups	3	25+
Standing calf	3	8
Crunches	3	25

DAY 2 (LIGHT)
Rest Period: 3 minutes
Repetition Maximum (RM): 85%

	Sets	Reps
Push press	4	6
Dead lift with hex bar	4	6
Medicine ball sit-up and twist	4	6
Pull-ups (modified if needed)	4	20+
Balance ball low abs	4	8
Low row	4	8
Shoulder raises with dumbbell	4	8
Dips (negative if needed)	4	10
Biceps curls	4	8
Wrist curls	4	10

DAY 3 (MEDIUM)
Rest Period: 3 minutes
Repetition Maximum (RM): 90%

	Sets	Reps
High pull	4	6
Bench press	4	10
Medicine ball lunge with twist to front leg	4	10
Twisting sit-ups	4	25+
Balance ball hamstrings	4	10
Step-ups	4	10

	Sets	Reps
Plyometric sit-ups (low abs)	4	10+
Pullover	4	10
Rotator cuff	4	15

WEEK 3
DAY 1 (HEAVY)

Rest Period: variable

Repetition Maximum (RM): 95% (for back squats, 85%-90%-95%-100%)

	Sets	Reps	Rest Period
Hang clean	4	6	1 minute
Back squats	4	8+	3 minutes
Incline press with dumbbell	4	8+	2 minutes
Romanian dead lift	4	8+	2 minutes
Leg curl (hamstrings)	4	8+	3 minutes
Single rows with dumbbell	4	8+	3 minutes
Side lunge	4	8+	2 minutes
Twisting sit-ups	4	25+	3 minutes
Standing calf	4	8+	3 minutes
Crunches	4	25+	2 minutes

DAY 2 (HEAVY)

Rest Period: variable

Repetition Maximum (RM): variable

	Sets	Reps	Rest Period	RM
Push press	4	6	3 minutes	85%-90%-95%-100%
Dead lift with hex bar	4	6	3 minutes	85%-90%-95%-100%
Medicine ball sit-up and twist	4	20+	2 minutes	
Pull-ups (modified if needed)	4	8+	2 minutes	
Balance ball low abs	4	8+	3 minutes	
Low row	4	8+	2 minutes	100%
Shoulder raises with dumbbell	4	8+	2 minutes	100%
Dips (negative if needed)	4	10+	2 minutes	
Biceps curls	4	8+	2 minutes	100%
Wrist curls	4	10+	2 minutes	100%

DAY 3 (LIGHT)

Rest Period: variable

Repetition Maximum (RM): 85%

DAY 3 (LIGHT) (continued)

	Sets	Reps	Rest Period
High pull	4	6	3 minutes
Bench press	4	10	3 minutes
Medicine ball lunge with twist to front leg	4	10	3 minutes
Twisting sit-ups	4	25+	3 minutes
Balance ball hamstrings	4	10	2 minutes
Step-ups	4	10	2 minutes
Plyometric sit-ups (low abs)	4	10+	2 minutes
Pullover	4	10	2 minutes
Rotator cuff	4	15	2 minutes

WEEK 4

DAY 1 (MEDIUM)

Rest Period: 2 minutes (3 minutes for back squat)
Repetition Maximum (RM): 90%

	Sets	Reps	Rest Period
Hang clean	4	6	3 minutes
Back squats	4	10-8-6-4	3 minutes
Incline press with dumbbell	4	10-8-6-4	2 minutes
Romanian dead lift	4	10-8-6-4	2 minutes
Leg curl (hamstrings)	4	10-8-6-4	2 minutes
Single rows with dumbbell	4	10-8-6-4	2 minutes
Side lunge	4	10-8-6-4	2 minutes
Twisting sit-ups	4	30-25-25-25+	2 minutes
Standing calf	4	10-8-6-4	2 minutes
Crunches	4	30-25-25-25+	2 minutes

DAY 2 (MEDIUM)

Rest Period: variable
Repetition Maximum (RM): 90%

	Sets	Reps	Rest Period
Push press	4	6-5-4-3	3 minutes
Dead lift with hex bar	4	6-5-4-3	3 minutes
Medicine ball sit-up and twist	3	25-25-20	2 minutes
Pull-ups (modified if needed)	3	10	2 minutes
Balance ball lower abs	4	10	2 minutes
Low row	4	10-8-6-4	2 minutes
Shoulder raises with dumbbell	4	10-8-6-4	2 minutes
Dips (neg. if needed)	3	10	2 minutes

	Sets	Reps	Rest Period
Biceps curls	3	10-8-6	2 minutes
Wrist curls	3	10	2 minutes

DAY 3 (HEAVY)

Rest Period: 2 minutes (3 minutes for high pull)
Repetition Maximum (RM): 100%

	Sets	Reps	Rest Period
High pull	4	6-5-4-2+	3 minutes
Bench press	4	6+	2 minutes
Medicine ball lunge with twist to front leg	4	10+	2 minutes
Twisting sit-ups	4	30-30-25-25+	2 minutes
Balance ball hamstrings	3	8+	2 minutes
Step-ups	3	10-8-6+	2 minutes
Plyometric sit-ups	3	15-15-10+	2 minutes
Pullover	3	10+	2 minutes
Rotator cuff	3	10	2 minutes

WEEK 5

DAY 1 (HEAVY)

Rest Period: 2 minutes (3 minutes for back squat)
Repetition Maximum (RM): 100%

	Sets	Reps	Rest Period
Hang clean	3	6	3 minutes
Back squats	3	7+	3 minutes
Incline press with dumbbell	3	7+	2 minutes
Romanian dead lift	3	7+	2 minutes
Leg curl (hamstrings)	3	7+	2 minutes
Single rows with dumbbell	3	7+	2 minutes
Side lunge	3	7+	2 minutes
Twisting sit-ups	3	30-25-25+	2 minutes
Standing calf	3	7+	2 minutes
Crunches	3	30-25-25+	2 minutes

DAY 2 (MEDIUM)

Rest Period: variable
Repetition Maximum (RM): 95%

	Sets	Reps	Rest Period
Push press	3	6	3 minutes
Dead lift with hex bar	3	6	3 minutes
Medicine ball sit-up and twist	3	25	2 minutes

DAY 2 (MEDIUM) (continued)

	Sets	Reps	Rest Period
Pull-ups (modified if needed)	3	12	2 minutes
Balance ball low abs	3	12	2 minutes
Low row	3	7	2 minutes
Shoulder raises with dumbbell	3	8	2 minutes
Dips (negative if needed)	3	12	2 minutes
Biceps curls	3	8	2 minutes
Wrist curls	3	10	2 minutes

DAY 3 (MEDIUM)

Rest Period: variable
Repetition Maximum (RM): 90%

	Sets	Reps	Rest Period
High pull	3	6	3 minutes
Bench press	3	6	3 minutes
Medicine ball lunge with twist to front leg	3	10	3 minutes
Twisting sit-ups	3	30+	3 minutes
Balance ball hamstrings	3	10+	2 minutes
Step-ups	3	8	2 minutes
Plyometric sit-ups (low abs)	3	25	2 minutes
Pullover	3	10	2 minutes
Rotator cuff	3	10	2 minutes

WEEK 6

DAY 1 (LIGHT)

Rest Period: 2 minutes
Repetition Maximum (RM): 85% (70% for practice hang clean)

	Sets	Reps	Rest Period
Hang clean	3	6	2 minutes
Back squats	3	6	2 minutes
Incline press with dumbbell	3	6	2 minutes
Romanian dead lift	3	6	2 minutes
Leg curl (hamstrings)	3	8	2 minutes
Single rows with dumbbell	3	6	2 minutes
Side lunge	3	8	2 minutes
Twisting sit-ups	3	30	2 minutes
Standing calf	3	8	2 minutes
Crunches	3	35-30-30	2 minutes

DAY 2 (MEDIUM)

Rest Period: variable
Repetition Maximum (RM): 90%

	Sets	Reps	Rest Period
Push press	3	6	3 minutes
Dead lift with hex bar	3	6	3 minutes
Medicine ball sit-up and twist	3	30-30-25	2 minutes
Pull-ups (modified if needed)	3	12+	2 minutes
Balance ball low abs	3	12+	3 minutes
Low row	3	8	2 minutes
Shoulder raises with dumbbell	3	25-20-20	2 minutes
Dips (negative if needed)	3	15-12-10+	2 minutes
Biceps curls	3	8	2 minutes
Wrist curls	3	10	2 minutes

DAY 3 (HEAVY)

Rest Period: variable
Repetition Maximum (RM): 100%

	Sets	Reps	Rest Period
High pull	3	6	3 minutes
Bench press	3	6+	3 minutes
Medicine ball lunge with twist to front leg	3	8+	3 minutes
Twisting sit-ups	3	35-30-30+	3 minutes
Balance ball hamstrings	3	10+	2 minutes
Step-ups	3	8+	2 minutes
Plyometric sit-ups (low abs)	3	25	2 minutes
Pullover	3	10	2 minutes
Rotator cuff	3	10	2 minutes

POWER PROGRAM—5 WEEKS

New exercises

Back squat to squat jump

Dumbbell bench press to push-up with clap

Accelerated step-up

Alternate leg/arm twisting crunch

Hang clean to push press

Upper back pull-up from squat rack

One-leg squat to toe raise

Push-ups to T stance

Side lunge

Additional equipment

Step-up box

Balance ball

Parallel bars
Medicine ball

WEEK 1
DAY 1 (LIGHT)

	Sets	Reps	Rest Period	RM
Back squat/squat jump	3	5	4 minutes	80%
Bench press with dumbbell/				
push-up with clap	3	5	4 minutes	80%
Accelerated step-up	3	8	3 minutes	80%
Pull-ups (modified if needed)	3	10	3 minutes	
Balance ball hamstrings	3	12	2 minutes	
Alternate leg/arm twisting				
crunch	3	25+	2 minutes	

DAY 2 (MEDIUM)

	Sets	Reps	Rest Period	RM
Hang clean to push press	3	6	3 minutes	70%
Dead lift with hex bar	3	4	3 minutes	90%
Upper back pull-up from				
squat rack	3	10	3 minutes	
Crunches (with weight if able)	3	15+	2 minutes	
Shoulder raises with				
dumbbell	3	10-8-6	2 minutes	90%
Dips (negative if needed)	3	8	3 minutes	
Wrist curls	3	12	2 minutes	

DAY 3 (HEAVY)

	Sets	Reps	Rest Period	RM
One-leg squats to toe raise	3	12	3 minutes	
Push-ups to T stance	3	15+	2 minutes	
Side lunge	3	10+	3 minutes	100%
Medicine ball seated				
crunch twist	3	30+	2 minutes	
Romanian dead lift	3	6+	3 minutes	100%
Balance ball low abs	3	15+	2 minutes	
Rotator cuff	3	15	2 minutes	

WEEK 2
DAY 1 (MEDIUM)

	Sets	Reps	Rest Period	RM
Back squat/squat jump	3	5	4 minutes	90%
Bench press with dumbbell/				
push-up with clap	3	5	4 minutes	90%
Accelerated step-up	3	8	3 minutes	90%
Pull-ups (modified if needed)	3	10+	3 minutes	

	Sets	Reps	Rest Period
Balance ball hamstrings	3	12	2 minutes
Alternate leg/arm twisting crunch	3	25+	2 minutes

DAY 2 (HEAVY)

	Sets	Reps	Rest Period	RM
Hang clean to push press	3	6+	3 minutes	70%
Dead lift with hex bar	3	4+	3 minutes	100%
Upper back pull-up from squat rack	3	10+	3 minutes	
Crunches (with weight if able)	3	15+	2 minutes	
Shoulder raises with dumbbell	3	10-8-6+	2 minutes	100%
Dips (negative if needed)	3	8+	3 minutes	
Wrist curls	3	12+	2 minutes	

DAY 3 (LIGHT)

	Sets	Reps	Rest Period	RM
One-leg squats to toe raise	3	12	3 minutes	
Push-ups to T stance	3	15+	2 minutes	
Side lunge	3	10	3 minutes	85%
Medicine ball seated crunch twist	3	30+	2 minutes	
Romanian dead lift	3	6+	3 minutes	85%
Balance ball low abs	3	15+	2 minutes	
Rotator cuff	3	15	2 minutes	

WEEK 3
DAY 1 (HEAVY)

	Sets	Reps	Rest Period	RM
Back squat/squat jump	3	5	4 minutes	85%
Bench press with dumbbell/ push-up with clap	3	5	4 minutes	85%
Accelerated step-up	3	10-8-8+	3 minutes	85%
Pull-ups (modified if needed)	3	12-10-10+	3 minutes	
Balance ball hamstrings	3	15+	2 minutes	
Alternate leg/arm twisting crunch	3	30-25-25+	2 minutes	

DAY 2 (MEDIUM)

	Sets	Reps	Rest Period	RM
Hang clean to push press	3	6	3 minutes	70%
Dead lift with hex bar	3	4	3 minutes	90%

DAY 2 (MEDIUM) (continued)

	Sets	Reps	Rest Period	RM
Upper back pull-up from squat rack	3	10+	3 minutes	
Crunches (with weight if able)	3	15+	2 minutes	
Shoulder raises with dumbbell	3	10-8-6	2 minutes	90%
Dips (negative if needed)	3	10-8-8+	3 minutes	
Wrist curls	3	12	2 minutes	

DAY 3 (MEDIUM)

	Sets	Reps	Rest Period	RM
One-leg squats to toe raise	3	12	3 minutes	
Push-ups to T stance	3	15+	2 minutes	
Side lunge	3	10	3 minutes	90%
Medicine ball seated crunch twist	3	30+	2 minutes	
Romanian dead lift	3	6	3 minutes	90%
Balance ball low abs	3	15+	2 minutes	
Rotator cuff	3	15	2 minutes	

WEEK 4
DAY 1 (MEDIUM)

	Sets	Reps	Rest Period	RM
Back squat/squat jump	3	5	4 minutes	85%
Bench press with dumbbell/ push-up with clap	3	5	4 minutes	85%
Accelerated step-up	3	8	3 minutes	95%
Pull-ups (modified if needed)	3	12-12-10	3 minutes	
Balance ball hamstrings	3	15	2 minutes	
Alternate leg/arm twisting crunch	3	25+	2 minutes	

DAY 2 (HEAVY)

	Sets	Reps	Rest Period	RM
Hang clean to push press	3	6	3 minutes	75%
Dead lift with hex bar	3	4+	3 minutes	100%
Upper back pull-up from squat rack	3	15-10-10	3 minutes	
Crunches (with weight if able)	3	15+	2 minutes	
Shoulder raises with dumbbell	3	10-8-6+	2 minutes	100%
Dips (negative if needed)	3	10-10-8+	3 minutes	
Wrist curls	3	12+	2 minutes	

DAY 3 (MEDIUM)

	Sets	Reps	Rest Period	RM
One-leg squats to toe raise	3	15-15-12+	3 minutes	
Push-ups to T stance	3	15+	2 minutes	
Side lunge	3	10	3 minutes	90%
Medicine ball seated crunch twist	3	30+	2 minutes	
Romanian dead lift	3	6	3 minutes	90%
Balance ball low abs	3	15+	2 minutes	
Rotator cuff	3	15	2 minutes	

WEEK 5
DAY 1 (LIGHT)

	Sets	Reps	Rest Period	RM
Back squat/squat jump	3	4	4 minutes	85%
Bench press with dumbbell/ push-up with clap	3	4	4 minutes	85%
Accelerated step-up	3	6+	3 minutes	85%
Pull-ups (modified if needed)	3	15-15-10+	3 minutes	
Balance ball hamstrings	3	15+	2 minutes	
Alternate leg/arm twisting crunch	3	30-30-25+	2 minutes	

DAY 2 (MEDIUM)

	Sets	Reps	Rest Period	RM
Hang clean to push press	3	6	3 minutes	70%
Dead lift with hex bar	3	4	3 minutes	95%
Upper back pull-up from squat rack	3	15-15-10+	3 minutes	
Crunches (with weight if able)	3	20-20-15+	2 minutes	
Shoulder raises with dumbbell	3	10-8-6	2 minutes	95%
Dips (negative if needed)	3	10	3 minutes	
Wrist curls	3	12	2 minutes	

DAY 3 (HEAVY)

	Sets	Reps	Rest Period	RM
One-leg squats to toe raise	3	15+	3 minutes	
Push-ups to T stance	3	20-15-15+	2 minutes	
Side lunge	3	8+	3 minutes	100%
Medicine ball seated crunch twist	3	30+	2 minutes	
Romanian dead lift	3	6+	3 minutes	100%
Balance ball low abs	3	20-15-15+	2 minutes	
Rotator cuff	3	15	2 minutes	

9

SPORT-SPECIFIC PROGRAMS: FIELD HOCKEY

Although field hockey is largely an earthbound sport, field hockey players need just as much strength in their legs, hips, and torso as do volleyball or basketball players. The exercises described in this sample field hockey program are designed to increase functional strength in these areas as well as address specific movements.

One factor that sets field hockey apart from these other sports is that players spend a lot of time in a bent-over position. This requires strong quadriceps (thigh muscles), hamstrings and, especially, lower back muscles. Exercises such as squats, lunges, and the good morning exercise strengthen these areas. Exercises using a balance ball, as well as one-leg squats to a toe raise, help develop balance and coordination.

Exercises using a medicine ball, such as twisting sit-ups, twisting lunges, and trunk twists, strengthen the trunk, arms, and shoulders, which can help you gain more power when you stroke the ball. Similarly, the pec fly/rear delt combination, which works the arms, shoulders and chest, simulates the stroking motion.

FIELD HOCKEY PROGRAM

New exercises

Medicine ball lunge with twist to front leg

Pec fly/rear delt

Push up to T stance

Dot drill

Additional equipment
Medicine ball
Mat for Dot drill

TRANSITION WEEK

DAY 1 (MEDIUM)

Rest Period: 3 minutes
Repetition Maximum (RM): 85%

	Sets	Reps
Agility drills		
Bench press	2	10
Leg curls (hamstrings)	2	10
Lat pulls (close grip)	2	10
Medicine ball seated side throw	2	12
Crunches	2	20
Biceps curls	2	12
Standing calf	2	12
Triceps	2	12

DAY 2 (MEDIUM)

Rest Period: 3 minutes
Repetition Maximum (RM): 85%

	Sets	Reps
Speed drills		
Medicine ball lunge with twist to front leg	2	12
Pec fly/rear delt	2	10
Seated leg curl	2	10
Low row	2	10
Seated calf	2	12
Standing row	2	12
Medicine ball seated twist	2	20
Triceps	2	12
Hip abduction/adduction	2	12

DAY 3 (MEDIUM)

Rest Period: 3 minutes
Repetition Maximum (RM): 85%

	Sets	Reps
Dot drill		
Push-up to T stance	2	15
Lat pulls (wide grip)	2	10

DAY 3 (MEDIUM) (continued)

	Sets	Reps
Hip abduction/adduction	2	10
Leg extension	2	12
Twisting sit-ups	2	20
Biceps curls	2	12
Crunches	2	20
Wrist curls	2	12

HYPERTROPHY PROGRAM—8 WEEKS

WEEK 1

DAY 1 (MEDIUM)

Rest Period: 3 minutes
Repetition Maximum (RM): 90%

	Sets	Reps
Agility drills		
Bench press	3	10
Leg curls (hamstrings)	3	10
Lat pulls (close grip)	3	10
Medicine ball seated side throw	3	20
Crunches	3	20
Biceps curls	3	12
Standing calf	3	12
Triceps	3	12

DAY 2 (MEDIUM)

Rest Period: 3 minutes (2 minutes for medicine ball lunge with twist to front leg)
Repetition Maximum (RM): 90%

	Sets	Reps
Speed drills		
Medicine ball lunge with twist to front leg	3	12-12-6
Pec fly/rear delt	3	10
Seated leg curl	3	10
Low row	3	10
Seated calf	3	12
Standing row	3	12
Medicine ball seated twist	3	20
Triceps	3	12
Hip abduction/adduction	3	12

DAY 3 (MEDIUM)
Rest Period: 3 minutes
Repetition Maximum (RM): 90%

	Sets	Reps
Dot drill		
Push-up to T stance	3	15
Lat pulls (wide grip)	3	10
Hip abduction/adduction	3	10
Leg extension	3	12
Twisting sit-ups	3	20
Biceps curls	3	12
Crunches	3	20
Wrist curl	3	12

WEEK 2
DAY 1 (HEAVY)
Rest Period: 3 minutes
Repetition Maximum (RM): 95%

	Sets	Reps
Agility drills		
Bench press	3	10+
Leg curls (hamstrings)	3	10+
Lat pulls (close grip)	3	10+
Medicine ball seated side throw	3	12+
Crunches	3	20+
Biceps curls	3	12+
Standing calf	3	12+
Triceps	3	12+

DAY 2 (LIGHT)
Rest Period: 3 minutes (2 minutes for medicine ball lunge with twist to front leg
Repetition Maximum (RM): 85%

	Sets	Reps
Speed drills		
Medicine ball lunge with twist to front leg	3	12
Pec fly/rear delt	3	10
Seated leg curl	3	10
Low row	3	10
Seated calf	3	12
Shoulder raises with dumbbell	3	12

DAY 2 (LIGHT) (continued)

	Sets	Reps
Medicine ball seated twist	3	20
Triceps	3	12
Hip abduction/adduction	3	12

DAY 3 (MEDIUM)
Rest Period: 3 minutes
Repetition Maximum (RM): 90%

	Sets	Reps
Dot drill		
Push-up to T stance	3	15
Lat pulls (wide grip)	3	10
Hip abduction/adduction	3	10
Leg extension	3	12
Twisting sit-ups	3	20
Biceps curls	3	12
Crunches	3	20
Wrist curls	3	12

WEEK 3
DAY 1 (HEAVY)
Rest Period: 3 minutes
Repetition Maximum (RM): 95%

	Sets	Reps
Form running drills		
Front squats	3	10+
Bench press	3	10+
Leg curls (hamstrings)	3	10+
Lat pulls (close grip)	3	10+
Twisting sit-ups	3	20+
Shoulder raises with dumbbell	3	12+
Crunches	3	20+
Biceps curls	3	12+
Standing calf	3	12+
Triceps	3	12+

DAY 2 (LIGHT)

Rest Period: 3 minutes
Repetition Maximum (RM): 85%

	Sets	Reps
Agility drills		
One-leg squat to cone touch	3	10

	Sets	Reps
Pec fly	3	10
Seated leg curl	3	10
Low row	3	10
Seated calf	3	12
Standing row	3	12
Medicine ball seated side throws	3	10
Triceps	3	12
Hip abduction/adduction	3	12
Wrist curls	3	12

DAY 3 (MEDIUM)

Rest Period: 3 minutes
Repetition Maximum (RM): 90%

	Sets	Reps
Dot drill		
Incline press	3	10
Lat pulls (wide grip)	3	10
Hip abduction/adduction	3	10
Pullover	3	12
Leg extension	3	12
Twisting sit-ups	3	20
Biceps curls	3	12
Crunches	3	20
Wrist curls	3	12

WEEK 4

DAY 1 (HEAVY)

Rest Period: 2 minutes
Repetition Maximum (RM): variable

	Sets	Reps	RM
Form running drills			
Bench press	4	10	85%-90%-95%-100%
Leg curls (hamstrings)	3	10+	85%
Lat pulls (close grip)	3	10+	100%
Medicine ball seated side throw	3	14+	100%
Crunches	3	20+	100%
Biceps curls	3	10+	100%
Standing calf	3	10+	100%
Triceps	3	10+	100%

DAY 2 (MEDIUM)

Rest Period: 2 minutes
Repetition Maximum (RM): 90%

DAY 2 (MEDIUM) (continued)

	Sets	Reps
Speed drills		
Medicine ball lunge with twist to front leg	4	12
Pec fly/rear delt	3	10
Seated leg curl	3	10
Low row	3	10
Seated calf	3	10
Shoulder raises with dumbbell	3	10
Medicine ball seated twist	3	20
Triceps	3	10
Hip abduction/adduction	3	10

DAY 3 (LIGHT)

Rest Period: 2 minutes
Repetition Maximum (RM): 85%

	Sets	Reps
Dot drill		
Push-up to T stance	4	20-15-10-10
Lat pulls (wide grip)	4	10
Hip abduction/adduction	3	10
Leg extension	3	10
Twisting sit-ups	3	20
Biceps curls	3	10
Crunches	3	20
Wrist curls	3	10

WEEK 5

DAY 1 (MEDIUM)

Rest Period: variable
Repetition Maximum (RM): 90%

	Sets	Reps	Rest Period
Agility drills			
Bench press	4	10	2 minutes
Leg curls (hamstrings)	3	10	1 minute
Lat pulls (close grip)	3	10	2 minutes
Seated medicine ball side throw	3	14	2 minutes
Crunches	3	20	1 minute
Biceps curls	3	10	1 minute
Standing calf	3	10	1 minute
Triceps	3	10	1 minute

DAY 2 (MEDIUM)

Rest Period: variable
Repetition Maximum (RM): 90%

	Sets	Reps	Rest Period
Speed drills			
Medicine ball lunge with twist to front leg	4	15-15-12-12	2 minutes
Pec fly/rear delt	3	10	2 minutes
Seated leg curl	3	10	2 minutes
Low row	3	10	2 minutes
Seated calf	3	10	1 minute
Shoulder raises with dumbbell	3	10	1 minute
Medicine ball seated twist	3	20	1 minute
Triceps	3	10	1 minute
Hip abduction/adduction	3	10	1 minute

DAY 3 (MEDIUM)

Rest Period: variable
Repetition Maximum (RM): 100%

	Sets	Reps	Rest Period
Dot drill			
Push-up to T stance	4	20-20-20-12	2 minutes
Lat pulls (wide grip)	3	10	2 minutes
Hip abduction/adduction	3	10+	1 minute
Leg extension	3	10+	1 minute
Twisting sit-ups	3	10+	1 minute
Biceps curls	3	10+	1 minute
Crunches	3	20	1 minute
Wrist curls	3	10+	1 minute

WEEK 6

DAY 1 (MEDIUM)

Rest Period: 1 minute
Repetition Maximum (RM): 90%

	Sets	Reps
Agility drills		
Bench press	4	10
Lat pulls (close grip)	3	10
Leg curls (hamstrings)	3	10
Medicine ball seated side throw	3	14
Standing row	3	10
Crunches	3	20

DAY 1 (MEDIUM) (continued)

	Sets	Reps
Biceps curls	3	10
Triceps	3	10

DAY 2 (HEAVY)

Rest Period: variable
Repetition Maximum (RM): variable

	Sets	Reps	Rest Period	RM
Speed drills				
Medicine ball lunge with twist to front leg	3	15	2 minutes	
Pec fly/rear delt	3	10	1 minute	100%
Seated leg curl	3	10	1 minute	100%
Low row	4	10	2 minutes	85%-90%-95%-100%
Seated calf	3	10+	1 minute	100%
Shoulder raises with dumbbell	3	10+	1 minute	100%
Medicine ball seated twist	3	20+	1 minute	
Triceps	3	10+	1 minute	100%
Hip abduction/adduction	3	10+	1 minute	100%

DAY 3 (MEDIUM)

Rest Period: 1 minute
Repetition Maximum (RM): 90%

	Sets	Reps
Dot drill		
Push-up to T stance	4	10
Lat pulls (wide grip)	4	10
Hip abduction/adduction	3	10
Leg extension	3	10
Twisting sit-ups	3	20
Biceps curls	3	10
Crunches	3	20
Wrist curls	3	10

WEEK 7

DAY 1 (HEAVY)

Rest Period: 1 minute (2 minutes for bench press)
Repetition Maximum (RM): variable

	Sets	Reps	RM
Agility drills			
Bench press	4	10	85%-90%-95%-100%
Lat pulls (close grip)	3	10+	100%
Leg curls (hamstrings)	4	10	100%
Medicine ball seated side throw	3	14+	
Standing row	3	10+	100%
Crunches	3	10+	
Biceps curls	3	10+	100%
Back extension	3	20+	100%
Triceps	3	10+	100%

DAY 2 (MEDIUM)

Rest Period: 1 minute
Repetition Maximum (RM): 90%

	Sets	Reps	Rest Period
Speed drills			
Medicine ball lunge with twist to front leg	4	15	1 minute
Pec fly/rear delt	4	10	1 minute
Low row	4	10	1 minute
Shoulder raises with dumbbell	3	10	1 minute
Seated leg curl	3	10	1 minute
Hip abduction/adduction	3	10	1 minute
Seated calf	3	10	1 minute
Medicine ball seated side throw	3	20	1 minute
Triceps	3	10	1 minute
Low back extension on machine	3	10	1 minute

DAY 3 (HEAVY)

Rest Period: variable
Repetition Maximum (RM): variable

	Sets	Reps	Rest Period	RM
Dot drill				
Push-up to T stance	4	10	2 minutes	
Lat pulls (wide grip)	4	10	2 minutes	85%-90%-95%-100%
Hip abduction/ adduction	4	12+	1 minute	100%
Leg extension	3	10+	1 minute	100%
Twisting sit-ups	3	20+	1 minute	
Biceps curls	3	10+	1 minute	100%
Crunches	3	20+	1 minute	
Good morning	3	10+	1 minute	100%
Wrist curls	3	10	1 minute	

WEEK 8
DAY 1 (MEDIUM)

Rest Period: 1 minute
Repetition Maximum (RM): 90%

	Sets	Reps
Agility drills		
Bench press	3	10
Lat pulls (close grip)	3	10
Leg curls (hamstrings)	3	10
Medicine ball seated side throw	3	14
Standing row	3	10
Crunches	3	10
Biceps curls	3	10
Back extension	3	20
Triceps	3	10

DAY 2 (MEDIUM)

Rest Period: 1 minute
Repetition Maximum (RM): 90%

	Sets	Reps
Speed drills		
Medicine ball lunge with twist to front leg	3	18-15-15
Pec fly/rear delt	3	10
Low row	3	10
Shoulder raises with dumbbell	3	10
Seated leg curl	3	10
Hip abduction/adduction	3	10
Seated calf	3	10
Medicine ball seated twist	3	20
Triceps	3	10
Low back extension on machine	3	10

DAY 3 (MEDIUM)

Rest Period: 1 minute
Repetition Maximum (RM): 85%

	Sets	Reps
Dot drill		
Incline press	3	10
Lat pulls (wide grip)	3	10
Pullover	3	10
Hip abduction/adduction	3	10
Leg extension	3	10
Twisting sit-ups	3	20
Biceps curls	3	10

	Sets	Reps
Crunches	3	20
Good morning	3	10
Wrist curls	3	10

STRENGTH PROGRAM—6 WEEKS

New exercises

Back squats

Push-ups on balance ball

Standing medicine ball foot toss

Side lunge

Medicine ball sit-up and twist

Medicine ball lunge with twist to front leg

Sitting medicine ball foot toss

Good morning

Medicine ball trunk twist

Additional equipment

Balance ball

Medicine ball

Ropes or cloth ladder

Chin-up bar

Parallel bars

WEEK 1
DAY 1 (MEDIUM)

Rest Period: 3 minutes
Repetition Maximum (RM): 90%

	Sets	Reps
Back squats	3	8
Push-ups on balance ball	3	8
Romanian dead lift	3	8
Standing medicine ball foot toss (butt kick)	3	8
Side lunge	3	8
Twisting sit-ups	3	25+
Standing calf	3	8
Crunches	3	25

DAY 2 (MEDIUM)

Rest Period: 3 minutes
Repetition Maximum (RM): 90%

	Sets	Reps
Dead lift with hex bar	3	6
Medicine ball sit-up and twist	3	6
Pull-ups (modified if needed)	3	20+
Balance ball low abs	3	8
Low row	3	8
Shoulder raises with dumbbell	3	8
Dips (negative if needed)	3	10
Biceps curls	3	8

DAY 3 (MEDIUM)

Rest Period: 3 minutes
Repetition Maximum (RM): 90%

	Sets	Reps
Dot drill		
Bench press	3	10
Medicine ball lunge with twist to front leg	3	10
Twisting sit-ups	3	25+
Balance ball hamstrings	3	10
Sitting medicine ball foot toss	3	10
Plyometric sit-ups (low abs)	3	10+
Good morning	3	10
Medicine ball trunk twist	3	15

WEEK 2

DAY 1 (MEDIUM)

Rest Period: 3 minutes
Repetition Maximum (RM): 90%

	Sets	Reps
Back squats	4	8
Push-ups on balance ball	4	8
Romanian dead lift	4	8
Standing medicine ball foot toss (butt kick)	4	8
Side lunge	4	8
Twisting sit-ups	4	25+
Standing calf	4	8
Crunches	4	25

DAY 2 (LIGHT)

Rest Period: 3 minutes
Repetition Maximum (RM): 85%

	Sets	Reps
Dead lift with hex bar	4	6
Medicine ball sit-up and twist	4	6
Pull-ups (modified if needed)	4	20+
Balance ball low abs	4	8
Low row	4	8
Shoulder raises with dumbbell	4	8
Dips (negative if needed)	4	10
Biceps curls	4	8

DAY 3 (MEDIUM)

Rest Period: 3 minutes
Repetition Maximum (RM): 90%

	Sets	Reps
Dot drill		
Bench press	4	10
Medicine ball lunge with twist to front leg	4	10
Twisting sit-ups	4	25+
Balance ball hamstrings	4	10
Sitting medicine ball foot toss	4	10
Plyometric sit-ups (low abs)	4	10+
Good morning	4	10
Medicine ball trunk twist	4	15

WEEK 3

DAY 1 (MEDIUM)

Rest Period: 3 minutes
Repetition Maximum (RM): 95%

	Sets	Reps
Agility drill		
Back squats	4	8
Push-ups on balance ball	4	8
Romanian dead lift	4	8
Standing medicine ball foot toss (butt kick)	4	8
Side lunge	4	8
Twisting sit-ups	4	25+
Standing calf	4	8
Crunches	4	25

DAY 2 (HEAVY)

Rest Period: variable
Repetition Maximum (RM): variable

	Sets	Reps	Rest Period	RM
Dead lift with hex bar	4	6	3 minutes	85%-90%-95%-100%
Medicine ball sit-up and twist	4	20+	2 minutes	
Pull-ups (modified if needed)	4	8+	3 minutes	
Balance ball low abs	4	8+	2 minutes	
Low row	4	8+	2 minutes	100%
Shoulder raises with dumbbell	4	8+	2 minutes	100%
Dips (negative if needed)	4	10+	2 minutes	
Biceps curls	4	8+	2 minutes	100%

DAY 3 (LIGHT)

Rest Period: variable
Repetition Maximum (RM): 85%

	Sets	Reps	Rest Period
Dot drill			
Bench press	4	10	3 minutes
Medicine ball lunge with twist to front leg	4	10	2 minutes
Twisting sit-ups	4	25+	3 minutes
Balance ball hamstrings	4	10	2 minutes
Sitting medicine ball foot toss	4	10	2 minutes
Plyometric sit-ups (low abs)	4	10+	2 minutes
Good morning	4	10	2 minutes
Medicine ball trunk twist	4	15	2 minutes

WEEK 4

DAY 1 (MEDIUM)

Rest Period: 2 minutes (3 minutes for back squats)
Repetition Maximum (RM): 90%

	Sets	Reps
Agility drill		
Back squats	4	10-8-6-4
Push-ups on balance ball	4	10-8-6-4
Romanian dead lift	4	10-8-6-4
Standing medicine ball foot toss (butt kick)	4	10-8-6-4

	Sets	Reps
Side lunge	4	10-8-6-4
Twisting sit-ups	4	25+
Standing calf	4	10-8-6-4
Crunches	4	25

DAY 2 (MEDIUM)

Rest Period: 2 minutes (3 minutes for dead lift)
Repetition Maximum (RM): 90%

	Sets	Reps
Dead lift with hex bar	4	6-5-4-3
Medicine ball sit-up and twist	3	25-25-20
Pull-ups (modified if needed)	3	10
Balance ball low abs	4	10
Low row	4	10-8-6-4
Shoulder raises with dumbbell	4	10-8-6-4
Dips (negative if needed)	3	10
Biceps curls	3	10-8-6

DAY 3 (HEAVY)

Rest Period: 2 minutes
Repetition Maximum (RM): 100%

	Sets	Reps
Dot drill		
Bench press	4	6+
Medicine ball lunge with twist to front leg	4	10+
Twisting sit-ups	4	25+
Balance ball hamstrings	3	8+
Sitting medicine ball foot toss	3	10+
Plyometric sit-ups (low abs)	3	10+
Good morning	3	10+
Medicine ball trunk twist	3	10

WEEK 5

DAY 1 (HEAVY)

Rest Period: 2 minutes (3 minutes for back squats)
Repetition Maximum (RM): 100%

	Sets	Reps
Agility drill		
Back squats	3	7+
Push-ups on balance ball	3	7+

DAY 1 (HEAVY) (continued)

	Sets	Reps
Romanian dead lift	3	7+
Standing medicine ball foot toss (butt kick)	3	7+
Side lunge	3	7+
Twisting sit-ups	3	25+
Standing calf	3	7+
Crunches	3	25

DAY 2 (MEDIUM)

Rest Period: 2 minutes (3 minutes for dead lift)
Repetition Maximum (RM): 95%

	Sets	Reps
Dead lift with hex bar	3	6
Medicine ball sit-up and twist	3	25
Pull-ups (modified if needed)3	12	
Balance ball low abs	3	12
Low row	3	7
Shoulder raises with dumbbell	3	8
Dips (negative if needed)3	12	
Biceps curls	3	8

DAY 3 (MEDIUM)

Rest Period: variable
Repetition Maximum (RM): 90%

	Sets	Reps	Rest Period
Dot drill			
Bench press	3	6	3 minutes
Medicine ball lunge with twist to front leg	3	15-15-10	3 minutes
Twisting sit-ups	3	30+	3 minutes
Balance ball hamstrings	3	10+	2 minutes
Sitting medicine ball foot toss	3	15	2 minutes
Plyometric sit-ups (low abs)	3	25	2 minutes
Good morning	3	10	2 minutes
Medicine ball trunk twist	3	10	2 minutes

WEEK 6

DAY 1 (LIGHT)

Rest Period: 2 minutes
Repetition Maximum (RM): 85%

	Sets	Reps
Agility drill		
Back squats	3	6
Push-ups on balance ball	3	6
Romanian dead lift	3	6
Standing medicine ball foot toss		
(butt kick)	3	8
Side lunge	3	8
Twisting sit-ups	3	30
Standing calf	3	8
Crunches	3	30

DAY 2 (MEDIUM)

Rest Period: variable
Repetition Maximum (RM): 90%

	Sets	Reps	Rest Period
Dead lift with hex bar	3	6	3 minutes
Medicine ball sit-up			
and twist	3	25	3 minutes
Pull-ups (modified if needed)	3	12+	2 minutes
Balance ball low abs	3	12+	3 minutes
Low row	3	8	2 minutes
Shoulder raises with			
dumbbell	3	25-25-20	2 minutes
Dips (negative if needed)	3	15-12-10+	2 minutes
Biceps curls	3	8	2 minutes

DAY 3 (HEAVY)

Rest Period: variable
Repetition Maximum (RM): variable

	Sets	Reps	Rest Period	RM
Dot drill				
Bench press	3	6+	3 minutes	90%-95%-100%
Medicine ball lunge with				
twist to front leg	3	15+	3 minutes	100%
Twisting sit-ups	3	30+	3 minutes	
Balance ball hamstrings	3	10+	2 minutes	100%
Sitting medicine ball				
foot toss	3	15+	2 minutes	
Plyometric sit-ups				
(low abs)	3	25	2 minutes	
Good morning	3	10	2 minutes	100%
Medicine ball trunk twist	3	10	2 minutes	

POWER PROGRAM—5 WEEKS

New exercises

Back squat/squat jump

Bench press/push-up with clap

Lunge jumps

Upper back pull-up from squat rack

One-leg squats to toe raise

Push-ups to T stance

Side lunge

Medicine ball seated crunch twist

Additional equipment

Medicine ball

Balance ball

Parallel bars

Chin-up bar

WEEK 1
DAY 1 (LIGHT)

	Sets	Reps	Rest Period	RM
Back squat/squat jump	3	5	4 minutes	85%
Bench press/push-up with clap	3	5	4 minutes	85%
Lunge jumps	3	7	3 minutes	
Pull-ups (modified if needed)	3	10	3 minutes	
Balance ball hamstrings	3	12	2 minutes	
Alternate leg/arm twisting crunch	3	25+	2 minutes	

DAY 2 (MEDIUM)

	Sets	Reps	Rest Period	RM
Hang clean	3	6	3 minutes	70%
Dead lift with hex bar	3	4	3 minutes	95%
Upper back pull-up from squat rack	3	10	3 minutes	
Crunches (with weight if able)	3	15+	2 minutes	
Shoulder raises with dumbbell	3	6	2 minutes	95%
Dips (negative if needed)	3	8	3 minutes	

DAY 3 (HEAVY)

	Sets	Reps	Rest Period	RM
One-leg squats to toe raise	3	12	3 minutes	
Push-ups to T stance	3	15+	2 minutes	
Side lunge	3	10+	3 minutes	100%
Medicine ball seated crunch twist	3	30+	2 minutes	
Romanian dead lift	3	6+	3 minutes	100%
Balance ball low abs	3	15+	2 minutes	

WEEK 2
DAY 1 (MEDIUM)

	Sets	Reps	Rest Period	RM
Back squat/squat jump	3	5	4 minutes	85%
Bench press/push-up with clap	3	5	4 minutes	85%
Lunge jumps	3	8	3 minutes	90%
Pull-ups (modified if needed)	3	10+	3 minutes	
Balance ball hamstrings	3	12	2 minutes	
Alternate leg/arm twisting crunch	3	25+	2 minutes	

DAY 2 (HEAVY)

	Sets	Reps	Rest Period	RM
Hang clean	3	6+	3 minutes	70%
Dead lift with hex bar	3	4+	3 minutes	100%
Upper back pull-up from squat rack	3	10+	3 minutes	
Crunches (with weight if able)	3	15+	2 minutes	
Shoulder raises with dumbbell	3	6+	2 minutes	100%
Dips (negative if needed)	3	8+	3 minutes	

DAY 3 (LIGHT)

	Sets	Reps	Rest Period	RM
One-leg squats to toe raise	3	12	3 minutes	
Push-ups to T stance	3	15+	2 minutes	
Side lunge	3	10	3 minutes	85%
Medicine ball seated crunch twist	3	30+	2 minutes	
Romanian dead lift	3	6+	3 minutes	85%
Balance ball low abs	3	15+	2 minutes	

WEEK 3
DAY 1 (HEAVY)

	Sets	Reps	Rest Period	RM
Back squat/squat jump	3	5	4 minutes	85%
Bench press/push-up with clap	3	5	4 minutes	85%
Lunge jumps	3	8+	3 minutes	100%
Pull-ups (modified if needed)	3	12-10-10+	3 minutes	
Balance ball hamstrings	3	15+	2 minutes	
Alternate leg/arm twisting crunch	3	30-25-25+	2 minutes	

DAY 2 (MEDIUM)

	Sets	Reps	Rest Period	RM
Hang clean	3	6	3 minutes	70%
Dead lift with hex bar	3	4	3 minutes	90%
Upper back pull-up from squat rack	3	10+	3 minutes	
Crunches (with weight if able)	3	15+	2 minutes	
Shoulder raises with dumbbell	3	6	2 minutes	90%
Dips (negative if needed)	3	8+	3 minutes	
Wrist curls	3	12	2 minutes	90%

DAY 3 (MEDIUM)

	Sets	Reps	Rest Period	RM
One-leg squats to toe raise	3	12	3 minutes	
Push-ups to T stance	3	15	2 minutes	
Side lunge	3	10	3 minutes	90%
Medicine ball seated crunch twist	3	30+	2 minutes	
Romanian dead lift	3	6	3 minutes	90%
Balance ball low abs	3	15	2 minutes	

WEEK 4
DAY 1 (MEDIUM)

	Sets	Reps	Rest Period	RM
Back squat/squat jump	3	5	4 minutes	85%
Bench press/push-up with clap	3	5	4 minutes	85%
Lunge jumps	3	9	3 minutes	
Pull-ups (modified if needed)	3	10	3 minutes	
Balance ball hamstrings	3	15	2 minutes	
Alternate leg/arm twisting crunch	3	25+	2 minutes	

DAY 2 (HEAVY)

	Sets	Reps	Rest Period	RM
Hang clean	3	6	3 minutes	75%
Dead lift with hex bar	3	4+	3 minutes	100%
Upper back pull-up from squat rack	3	15-10-10	3 minutes	
Crunches (with weight if able)	3	15+	2 minutes	
Shoulder raises with dumbbell	3	10-8-6+	2 minutes	100%
Dips (negative if needed)	3	10-10-8+	3 minutes	
Wrist curls	3	12	2 minutes	

DAY 3 (MEDIUM)

	Sets	Reps	Rest Period	RM
One-leg squats to toe raise	3	15-15-12+	3 minutes	
Push-ups to T stance	3	15+	2 minutes	
Side lunge	3	10	3 minutes	95%
Medicine ball seated crunch twist	3	30+	2 minutes	
Romanian dead lift	3	6	3 minutes	95%
Balance ball low abs	3	15+	2 minutes	

WEEK 5
DAY 1 (HEAVY)

	Sets	Reps	Rest Period	RM
Back squat/squat jump	3	4	4 minutes	85%
Bench press/push-up with clap	3	4	4 minutes	85%
Lunge jumps	3	12	3 minutes	
Pull-ups (modified if needed)	3	10+	3 minutes	
Balance ball hamstrings	3	15+	2 minutes	
Alternate leg/arm twisting crunch	3	25+	2 minutes	

DAY 2 (MEDIUM)

	Sets	Reps	Rest Period	RM
Hang clean	3	6	3 minutes	70%
Dead lift with hex bar	3	4	3 minutes	95%
Upper back pull-up from squat rack	3	10+	3 minutes	
Crunches (with weight if able)	3	15+	2 minutes	
Shoulder raises with dumbbell	3	6	2 minutes	95%
Dips (negative if needed)	3	10	3 minutes	
Wrist curls	3	12	2 minutes	

DAY 3 (HEAVY)

	Sets	Reps	Rest Period	RM
One-leg squats to toe raise	3	15+	3 minutes	
Push-ups to T stance	3	20-15-15+	2 minutes	
Side lunge	3	8+	3 minutes	100%
Medicine ball seated				
crunchtwist	3	30+	2 minutes	
Romanian dead lift	3	6+	3 minutes	100%
Balance ball low abs	3	20-15-15+	2 minutes	

10
SPORT-SPECIFIC PROGRAMS: SOFTBALL

In addition to requiring basic functional strength, softball demands well-developed hand-eye coordination, balance, and explosiveness. Much of the power you produce when throwing and hitting, not to mention running and pivoting, comes from strength in your trunk, hips, and legs.

The specific exercises in the following programs address these areas. Medicine ball exercises develop the trunk and chest muscles, and hip abduction and adduction exercises aid when you are running laterally, as infielders and baserunners must do. One-leg squats to cone touch, featured in the Hypertrophy and Power phases, simulate a fielder running and picking up a ground ball. Exercises using a balance ball help with balance as well as power, and can come in handy when you are trying to make an off-balance throw. Ladder drills and speed drills develop speed, coordination, and balance required when fielding and running the bases. Finally, rotator cuff exercises strengthen the muscles around the shoulder, which probably absorbs the most stress of any joint.

SOFTBALL PROGRAM

New exercises
Form running drills
Agility drills
One-leg squat to cone touch
Medicine ball seated side throws
Dot drill

Additional equipment
Medicine ball
Mat for dot drill
Cones

TRANSITION WEEK

DAY 1 (MEDIUM)

Rest Period: 3 minutes
Repetition Maximum (RM): 85%

	Sets	Reps
Form running drills		
Front squats	2	10
Bench press	2	10
Leg curls (hamstrings)	2	10
Lat pulls (close grip)	2	10
Twisting sit-ups	2	20
Shoulder raises with dumbbell	2	12
Crunches	2	20
Biceps curls	2	12
Standing calf	2	12
Triceps	2	12

DAY 2 (MEDIUM)

Rest Period: 3 minutes
Repetition Maximum (RM): 85%

	Sets	Reps
Agility drills		
One-leg squat to cone touch	2	6
Pec fly	2	10
Seated leg curl	2	10
Low row	2	10
Seated calf	2	12
Standing row	2	12
Medicine ball seated side throws	2	10
Triceps	2	12
Hip abduction/adduction	2	12
Wrist curls	2	12

DAY 3 (MEDIUM)

Rest Period: 3 minutes
Repetition Maximum (RM): 85%

	Sets	Reps
Dot drill		
Incline press	2	10
Lat pulls (wide grip)	2	10
Hip abduction/adduction	2	10
Pullover	2	12
Leg extension	2	12
Twisting sit-ups	2	20
Biceps curls	2	12
Crunches	2	20
Wrist curls	2	12

HYPERTROPHY PROGRAM—8 WEEKS

WEEK 1
DAY 1 (MEDIUM)

Rest Period: 3 minutes
Repetition Maximum (RM): 90%

	Sets	Reps
Form running drills		
Front squats	3	10
Bench press	3	10
Leg curls (hamstrings)	3	10
Lat pulls (close grip)	3	10
Twisting sit-ups	3	20
Shoulder raises with dumbbell	3	12
Crunches	3	20
Biceps curls	3	12
Standing calf	3	12
Triceps	3	12

DAY 2 (MEDIUM)

Rest Period: 3 minutes
Repetition Maximum (RM): 90%

	Sets	Reps
Agility drills		
One-leg squat to cone touch	3	6
Pec fly	3	10
Seated leg curl	3	10
Low row	3	10
Seated calf	3	12
Standing row	3	12

DAY 2 (MEDIUM) (continued)

	Sets	Reps
Medicine ball seated side throws	3	10
Triceps	3	12
Hip abduction/adduction	3	12
Wrist curls	3	12

DAY 3 (MEDIUM)

Rest Period: 3 minutes
Repetition Maximum (RM): 90%

	Sets	Reps
Dot drill		
Incline press	3	10
Lat pulls (wide grip)	3	10
Hip abduction/adduction	3	10
Pullover	3	12
Leg extension	3	12
Twisting sit-ups	3	20
Biceps curls	3	12
Crunches	3	20
Wrist curls	3	12

WEEK 2

DAY 1 (HEAVY)

Rest Period: 3 minutes
Repetition Maximum (RM): 95%

	Sets	Reps
Form running drills		
Front squats	3	10+
Bench press	3	10+
Leg curls (hamstrings)	3	10+
Lat pulls (close grip)	3	10+
Twisting sit-ups	3	20+
Shoulder raises with dumbbell	3	12+
Crunches	3	20+
Biceps curls	3	12+
Standing calf	3	12+
Triceps	3	12+

DAY 2 (LIGHT)

Rest Period: 3 minutes
Repetition Maximum (RM): 85%

	Sets	Reps
Agility drills		
One-leg squat to cone touch	3	10
Pec fly	3	10
Seated leg curl	3	10
Low row	3	10
Seated calf	3	12
Standing row	3	12
Medicine ball seated side throws	3	10
Triceps	3	12
Hip abduction/adduction	3	12
Wrist curls	3	12

DAY 3 (MEDIUM)

Rest Period: 3 minutes
Repetition Maximum (RM): 90%

	Sets	Reps
Dot drill		
Incline press	3	10
Lat pulls (wide grip)	3	10
Hip abduction/adduction	3	10
Pullover	3	12
Leg extension	3	12
Twisting sit-ups	3	20
Biceps curls	3	12
Crunches	3	20
Wrist curls	3	12

WEEK 3
DAY 1 (LIGHT)

Rest Period: variable
Repetition Maximum (RM): 85%

	Sets	Reps	Rest Period
Form running drills			
Front squats	3	10	3 minutes
Bench press	3	10	3 minutes
Leg curls (hamstrings)	3	10	3 minutes
Lat pulls (close grip)	3	10	3 minutes
Twisting sit-ups	3	20	2 minutes
Shoulder raises with dumbbells	3	12	2 minutes
Crunches	3	20	2 minutes
Biceps curls	3	12	2 minutes
Standing calf	3	12	2 minutes
Triceps	3	12	2 minutes

DAY 2 (HEAVY)

Rest Period: variable
Repetition Maximum (RM): 100%

	Sets	Reps	Rest Period
Agility drills			
One-leg squat to cone touch	3	12-12-10+	3 minutes
Pec fly	3	10+	3 minutes
Seated leg curl	3	10+	3 minutes
Low row	3	10+	3 minutes
Seated calf	3	12+	2 minutes
Standing row	3	12+	2 minutes
Medicine ball seated side throws	3	12	2 minutes
Triceps	3	12+	2 minutes
Hip abduction/adduction	3	12+	2 minutes

DAY 3 (MEDIUM)

Rest Period: 3 minutes
Repetition Maximum (RM): 85%

	Sets	Reps	Rest Period
Dot drill			
Incline press	3	10	3 minutes
Lat pulls (wide grip)	3	10	3 minutes
Hip abduction/adduction	3	10	2 minutes
Pullover	3	12	2 minutes
Leg extension	3	12	2 minutes
Twisting sit-ups	3	20	2 minutes
Biceps curls	3	12	2 minutes
Crunches	3	20	2 minutes
Wrist curls	3	12	2 minutes

WEEK 4
DAY 1 (HEAVY)

Rest Period: 2 minutes
Repetition Maximum (RM): variable

	Sets	Reps	RM
Form running drills			
Front squats	4	10	85%-90%-95%-100%
Bench press	4	10	85%-90%-95%-100%

	Sets	Reps	RM
Leg curls (hamstrings)	3	10+	85%
Lat pulls (close grip)	3	10+	100%
Twisting sit-ups	3	20+	100%
Shoulder raises with dumbbell	3	10+	100%
Crunches	3	20+	100%
Biceps curls	3	10+	100%
Standing calf	3	10+	100%
Triceps	3	10+	100%

DAY 2 (MEDIUM)

Rest Period: 2 minutes
Repetition Maximum (RM): 90%

	Sets	Reps
Agility drills		
One-leg squat to cone touch	4	12-12-10-10
Pec fly	3	10
Seated leg curl	3	10
Low row	3	10
Seated calf	3	10
Standing row	3	10
Medicine ball seated side throws	3	12
Triceps	3	10
Hip abduction/adduction	3	10
Wrist curls	3	10

DAY 3 (LIGHT)

Rest Period: 2 minutes
Repetition Maximum (RM): 85%

	Sets	Reps
Dot drill		
Incline press	4	10
Lat pulls (wide grip)	4	10
Hip abduction/adduction	3	10
Pullover	3	10
Leg extension	3	10
Twisting sit-ups	3	20
Biceps curls	3	10
Crunches	3	20
Wrist curls	3	10

WEEK 5
DAY 1 (MEDIUM)

Rest Period: variable
Repetition Maximum (RM): 90%

	Sets	Reps	Rest Period
Form running drills			
Front squat	4	10	2 minutes
Bench press	4	10	2 minutes
Leg curls (hamstrings)	3	10	1 minute
Lat pulls (close grip)	3	10	2 minutes
Twisting sit-ups	3	20	1 minute
Shoulder raises with dumbbell	3	10	2 minutes
Crunches	3	20	1 minute
Biceps curls	3	10	1 minute
Standing calf	3	10	1 minute
Triceps	3	10	1 minute

DAY 2 (MEDIUM)

Rest Period: variable
Repetition Maximum (RM): 90%

	Sets	Reps	Rest Period
Agility drills			
One-leg squat to cone touch	4	12-12-12-10	2 minutes
Pec fly	3	10	2 minutes
Seated leg curl	3	10	2 minutes
Low row	3	10	2 minutes
Seated calf	3	10	1 minute
Standing row	3	10	1 minute
Medicine ball seated side throws	3	12	1 minute
Triceps	3	10	1 minute
Hip abduction/adduction	3	10	1 minute
Wrist curls	3	10	1 minute

DAY 3 (MEDIUM)

Rest Period: variable
Repetition Maximum (RM): variable

	Sets	Reps	Rest Period	RM
Dot drill				
Incline press	4	10	2 minutes	85%-90%-95%-100%
Lat pulls (wide grip)	4	10	2 minutes	85%-90%-95%-100%
Hip abduction/ adduction	3	10	1 minute	
Pullover	3	10+	1 minute	
Leg extension	3	10+	1 minute	
Twisting sit-ups	3	20	1 minute	
Biceps curls	3	10+	1 minute	
Crunches	3	20	1 minute	
Wrist curls	3	10+	1 minute	

WEEK 6

DAY 1 (MEDIUM)

Rest Period: 1 minute
Repetition Maximum (RM): 90%

	Sets	Reps
Form running drills		
Front squats	4	10
Bench press	4	10
Lat pulls (close grip)	3	10
Leg curls (hamstrings)	3	10
Standing calf	3	10
Twisting sit-ups	3	20
Standing row	3	10
Crunches	3	20
Biceps curls	3	10
Triceps	3	10

DAY 2 (HEAVY)

Rest Period: variable
Repetition Maximum (RM): variable

	Sets	Reps	Rest Period
Agility drills			
One-leg squat to cone touch	4	12	2 minutes

DAY 2 (HEAVY) (continued)

	Sets	Reps	Rest Period	RM
Pec fly	3	10	1 minute	100%
Seated leg curl	3	10	1 minute	100%
Low row	4	10	2 minutes	85%-90%-95%-100%
Seated calf	3	10+	1 minute	100%
Shoulder raises with dumbbell	3	10+	1 minute	100%
Medicine ball seated side throws	3	15-12-12	1 minute	
Triceps	3	10+	1 minute	100%
Hip abduction/ adduction	3	10+	1 minute	100%
Wrist curls	3	10+	1 minute	100%

DAY 3 (MEDIUM)

Rest Period: 1 minute
Repetition Maximum (RM): 90%

	Sets	Reps
Dot drill		
Incline press	4	10
Lat pulls (wide grip)	4	10
Hip abduction/adduction	3	10
Pullover	3	10
Leg extension	3	10
Twisting sit-ups	3	20
Biceps curls	3	10
Crunches	3	20
Wrist curls	3	10

WEEK 7
DAY 1 (HEAVY)

Rest Period: variable
Repetition Maximum (RM): variable

	Sets	Reps	Rest Period	RM
Form running drills				
Front squats	4	10	2 minutes	85%-90%-95%-100%
Bench press	4	10	2 minutes	85%-90%-95%-100%
Lat pulls (close grip)	3	10+	1 minute	100%

	Sets	Reps	Rest Period	RM
Leg curls (hamstrings)	4	10	1 minute	100%
Standing calf	3	10+	1 minute	100%
Twisting sit-ups	4	20-20-20-10	1 minute	
Standing row	3	10+	1 minute	100%
Crunches	3	10+	1 minute	
Biceps curls	3	10+	1 minute	100%
Back extension	3	20+	1 minute	100%
Triceps	3	10+	1 minute	100%

DAY 2 (MEDIUM)

Rest Period: variable
Repetition Maximum (RM): 90%

	Sets	Reps	Rest Period
Agility drills			
One-leg squat to cone touch	4	14-12-12-12	2 minutes
Pec fly	4	10	1 minute
Low row	4	10	1 minute
Shoulder raises with dumbbell	3	10	1 minute
Seated leg curl	3	10	1 minute
Hip abduction/adduction	3	10	1 minute
Seated calf	3	10	1 minute
Medicine ball seated side throws	3	15-15-12	1 minute
Triceps	3	10	1 minute
Wrist curls	3	10	1 minute

DAY 3 (HEAVY)

Rest Period: variable
Repetition Maximum (RM): variable

	Sets	Reps	Rest Period	RM
Dot drill				
Incline press	4	10	2 minutes	85%-90%-95%-100%
Lat pulls (wide grip)	4	10	2 minutes	85%-90%-95%-100%
Pullover	3	10+	1 minute	
Hip abduction/ adduction	3	10-10-10-12	1 minute	85%-90%-95%-100%
Leg extension	3	10+	1 minute	

DAY 3 (HEAVY) (continued)

	Sets	Reps	Rest Period
Twisting sit-ups	3	20+	1 minute
Biceps curls	3	10+	1 minute
Crunches	3	20+	1 minute
Good morning	3	10+	1 minute

WEEK 8
DAY 1 (MEDIUM)
Rest Period: 1 minute
Repetition Maximum (RM): 90%

	Sets	Reps
Form running drills		
Front squats	3	10
Bench press	3	10
Lat pulls (close grip)	3	10
Leg curls (hamstrings)	3	10
Standing calf	3	10
Twisting sit-ups	3	20
Standing row	3	10
Crunches	3	10
Biceps curls	3	10
Back extension	3	20
Triceps	3	10

DAY 2 (MEDIUM)
Rest Period: variable
Repetition Maximum (RM): 90%

	Sets	Reps	Rest Period
Agility drills			
One-leg squat to cone touch	3	14-14-12	2 minutes
Pec fly	3	10	1 minute
Low row	3	10	1 minute
Shoulder raises with dumbbell	3	10	1 minute
Seated leg curl	3	10	1 minute
Hip abduction/adduction	3	10	1 minute
Seated calf	3	10	1 minute
Medicine ball seated side throws	3	15-15-12	1 minute
Triceps	3	10	1 minute
Wrist curls	3	10	1 minute

DAY 3 (MEDIUM)

Rest Period: 1 minute
Repetition Maximum (RM): 85%

	Sets	Reps
Dot drill		
Incline press	3	10
Lat pulls (wide grip)	3	10
Pullover	3	10
Hip abduction/adduction	3	10
Leg extension	3	10
Twisting sit-ups	3	20
Biceps curls	3	10
Crunches	3	20
Good morning	3	10

STRENGTH PROGRAM—6 WEEKS

New exercises

Dumbbell incline press on balance ball

Standing medicine ball side throw

Chin-ups

Agility drills

Lunge with twist to front leg

Rotator cuff exercises

Additional equipment

Balance ball

Medicine ball

Chin-up bar

Parallel bars

Step-up box

WEEK 1

DAY 1 (MEDIUM)

Rest Period: 3 minutes
Repetition Maximum (RM): 90%

DAY 1 (MEDIUM) (continued)

	Sets	Reps
Back squats	3	8
Balance ball incline press with dumbbell	3	8
Single rows with dumbbell	3	8
Side lunge	3	8
Twisting sit-ups	3	25+
Standing calf	3	8
Crunches	3	25

DAY 2 (MEDIUM)

Rest Period: 3 minutes
Repetition Maximum (RM): 90%

	Sets	Reps
Dead lift with hex bar	3	6
Standing medicine ball side throw	3	20+
Pull-ups (modified if needed)	3	8
Balance ball low abs	3	10+
Chin-ups	3	8
Shoulder raises with dumbbell	3	10
Dips (negative if needed)	3	8
Wrist curls	3	10

DAY 3 (MEDIUM)

Rest Period: 3 minutes
Repetition Maximum (RM): 90%

	Sets	Reps
Agility drills		
Bench press	3	8
Medicine ball lunge with twist to front leg	3	10
Twisting sit-ups	3	25+
Balance ball hamstrings	3	10
Step-ups	3	10
Plyometric sit-ups (low abs)	3	10+
Pullover	3	10
Rotator cuff	3	15

WEEK 2
DAY 1 (MEDIUM)

Rest Period: 3 minutes
Repetition Maximum (RM): 90%

	Sets	Reps
Back squats	4	8
Balance ball incline press with dumbbell	4	8
Romanian dead lift	4	8
Single rows with dumbbell	4	8
Side lunge	4	8
Twisting sit-ups	4	25+
Standing calf	4	8
Crunches	4	25

DAY 2 (LIGHT)

Rest Period: 3 minutes
Repetition Maximum (RM): 85%

	Sets	Reps
Dead lift with hex bar	4	6
Standing medicine ball side throw	4	6
Pull-ups (modified if needed)	4	20+
Balance ball low abs	4	8
Chin-ups	4	8
Shoulder raises with dumbbell	4	8
Dips (negative if needed)	4	10
Wrist curls	4	10

DAY 3 (MEDIUM)

Rest Period: 3 minutes
Repetition Maximum (RM): 90%

	Sets	Reps
Agility drills		
Bench press	4	8-6-4-2
Medicine ball lunge with twist to front leg	4	10
Twisting sit-ups	4	25+
Balance ball hamstrings	4	10
Step-ups	4	10
Plyometric sit-ups (low abs)	4	10+
Pullover	4	10
Rotator cuff	4	15

WEEK 3

DAY 1 (MEDIUM)

Rest Period: variable
Repetition Maximum (RM): 95%

DAY 1 (MEDIUM) (continued)

	Sets	Reps	Rest Period
Back squats	4	8	3 minutes
Balance ball incline press with dumbbell	4	8	3 minutes
Romanian dead lift	4	8	2 minutes
Single rows with dumbbell	4	8	3 minutes
Side lunge	4	8	2 minutes
Twisting sit-ups	4	25+	3 minutes
Standing calf	4	8	3 minutes
Crunches	4	25	2 minutes

DAY 2 (HEAVY)

Rest Period: variable
Repetition Maximum (RM): variable

	Sets	Reps	Rest Period	RM
Dead lift with hex bar	4	6	3 minutes	85%-90%-95%-100%
Standing medicine ball side throw	4	25-20-20-20+		
Pull-ups (modified if needed)	4	8+	2 minutes	
Balance ball low abs	4	8+	3 minutes	
Chin-ups	4	8+	2 minutes	
Shoulder raise with dumbbell	4	8+	2 minutes	100%
Dips (negative if needed)	4	10+	2 minutes	
Wrist curls	4	10+	2 minutes	

DAY 3 (LIGHT)

Rest Period: variable
Repetition Maximum (RM): 85%

	Sets	Reps	Rest Period
Agility drills			
Bench press	4	6	3 minutes
Medicine ball lunge with twist to front leg	4	10	3 minutes
Twisting sit-ups	4	25+	3 minutes
Balance ball hamstrings	4	8	2 minutes
Step-ups	4	8	2 minutes
Plyometric sit-ups (low abs)	4	10	2 minutes
Pullover	4	10	2 minutes
Rotator cuff	4	10	2 minutes

WEEK 4
DAY 1 (MEDIUM)

Rest Period: variable
Repetition Maximum (RM): 90%

	Sets	Reps	Rest Period
Back squats	4	10-8-6-4	3 minutes
Balance ball incline press			
with dumbbell	4	10-8-6-4	2 minutes
Romanian dead lift	4	10-8-6-4	2 minutes
Single rows with			
dumbbell	4	10-8-6-4	2 minutes
Side lunge	4	10-8-6-4	2 minutes
Twisting sit-ups	4	30-25-25-25+	2 minutes
Standing calf	4	10-8-6-4	2 minutes
Crunches	4	30-25-25-25+	2 minutes

DAY 2 (MEDIUM)

Rest Period: variable
Repetition Maximum (RM): 90%

	Sets	Reps	Rest Period
Dead lift with hex bar	4	6-5-4-3	3 minutes
Standing medicine ball			
side throw	3	25-25-20	2 minutes
Pull-ups (modified if			
needed)	3	10	2 minutes
Balance ball low abs	4	10	2 minutes
Chin-ups	4	10-8-6-4	2 minutes
Shoulder raises with			
dumbbell	4	10-8-6-4	2 minutes
Dips (negative if			
needed)	3	10	2 minutes
Wrist curls	3	10	2 minutes

DAY 3 (HEAVY)

Rest Period: 2 minutes (3 minutes for agility drills)
Repetition Maximum (RM): 100%

	Sets	Reps
Agility drills		
Bench press	4	6+
Medicine ball lunge with		
twist to front leg	4	10+
Twisting sit-ups	4	30-30-25-25+

DAY 3 (HEAVY) (continued)

	Sets	Reps
Balance ball hamstrings	3	8+
Step-ups	3	10-8-6+
Plyometric sit-ups (low abs)	3	15-15-10+
Pullover	3	10+
Rotator cuff	3	10

WEEK 5
DAY 1 (HEAVY)

Rest Period: variable
Repetition Maximum (RM): 90%

	Sets	Reps	Rest Period
Back squats	3	7+	3 minutes
Balance ball incline press with dumbbell	3	7+	2 minutes
Romanian dead lift	3	7+	2 minutes
Single rows with dumbbell	3	7+	2 minutes
Side lunge	3	7+	2 minutes
Twisting sit-ups	3	30-25-25+	2 minutes
Standing calf	3	7+	2 minutes
Crunches	3	30-25-25+	2 minutes

DAY 2 (MEDIUM)

Rest Period: variable
Repetition Maximum (RM): 95%

	Sets	Reps	Rest Period
Dead lift with hex bar	3	6	3 minutes
Standing medicine ball side throw	3	25	2 minutes
Pull-ups (modified if needed)	3	12	2 minutes
Balance ball low abs	3	12	2 minutes
Chin-ups	3	7	2 minutes
Shoulder raises with dumbbell	3	8	2 minutes
Dips (negative if needed)	3	12	2 minutes
Wrist curls	3	10	2 minutes

DAY 3 (MEDIUM)

Rest Period: variable
Repetition Maximum (RM): 90%

	Sets	Reps	Rest Period
Agility drills			
Bench press	3	6	3 minutes
Medicine ball lunge with			
twist to front leg	3	10	3 minutes
Twisting sit-ups	3	30+	3 minutes
Balance ball hamstrings	3	10+	2 minutes
Step-ups	3	8	2 minutes
Plyometric sit-ups			
(low abs)	3	25	2 minutes
Pullover	3	10	2 minutes
Rotator cuff	3	10	2 minutes

WEEK 6
DAY 1 (LIGHT)

Rest Period: 2 minutes
Repetition Maximum (RM): 85% (70% for ladder drills)

	Sets	Reps
Back squats	3	6
Balance ball incline press		
with dumbbell	3	6
Romanian dead lift		
Single with dumbbell	3	6
Side lunge	3	8
Twisting sit-ups	3	30
Standing calf	3	8
Crunches	3	30

DAY 2 (MEDIUM)

Rest Period: variable
Repetition Maximum (RM): 90%

	Sets	Reps	Rest Period
Dead lift with hex bar	3	6	3 minutes
Standing medicine ball			
side throw	3	30-30-25	2 minutes
Pull-ups (modified if			
needed)	3	12+	3 minutes
Balance ball low abs	3	12+	2 minutes
Chin-ups	3	8	2 minutes
Shoulder raises with			
dumbbell	3	*25-20-20	2 minutes
Dips (negative if needed)	3	*15-12-10	2 minutes
Wrist curls	3	10	2 minutes

DAY 3 (HEAVY)

Rest Period: variable
Repetition Maximum (RM): variable

	Sets	Reps	Rest Period	RM
Agility drills				
Bench press	3	6+	3 minutes	90%
Medicine ball lunge with				
twist to front leg	3	8+	3 minutes	100%
Twisting sit-ups	3	30+	3 minutes	
Balance ball hamstrings	3	10+	2 minutes	100%
Step-ups	3	8+	2 minutes	100%
Plyometric sit-ups				
(low abs)	3	*25	2 minutes	
Pullover	3	10	2 minutes	
Rotator cuff	3	10	2 minutes	100%

POWER PROGRAM—5 WEEKS

New exercises

Front squat to squat jump

Balance ball push-ups to push-up with clap

Accelerated step-up

Alternate leg/arm twisting crunch

Upper back pull-up from squat rack

One-leg squats to cone touch

Push-ups to T stance

Side lunge

Medicine ball seated crunch twist

Additional equipment

Chin-up bar

Parallel bars

Balance ball

Medicine ball

Step-up box

Cones

WEEK 1
DAY 1 (LIGHT)

	Sets	Reps	Rest Period	RM
Front squat/squat jump	3	5	4 minutes	85%
Balance ball push-up/ push-up with clap	3	5	4 minutes	85%
Accelerated step-ups	3	8	3 minutes	85%
Pull-ups (modified if needed)	3	10	3 minutes	
Balance ball hamstrings	3	12	2 minutes	
Alternate leg/arm twisting crunch	3	25+	2 minutes	

DAY 2 (MEDIUM)

	Sets	Reps	Rest Period	RM
Hang clean	3	6	3 minutes	70%
Dead lift with hex bar	3	4	3 minutes	95%
Upper back pull-up from squat rack	3	10	3 minutes	
Crunches (with weight if able)	3	15+	2 minutes	
Shoulder raises with dumbbell	3	10-8-6	2 minutes	95%
Dips (negative if needed)	3	8	3 minutes	
Wrist curls	3	12	2 minutes	

DAY 3 (HEAVY)

	Sets	Reps	Rest Period	RM
One-leg squats to cone touch	3	12	3 minutes	
Push-ups to T stance	3	15+	2 minutes	
Side lunge	3	10+	3 minutes	100%
Medicine ball seated crunch twist	3	30+	2 minutes	
Romanian dead lift	3	6+	3 minutes	100%
Balance ball low abs	3	15+	2 minutes	
Rotator cuff	3	15	2 minutes	

WEEK 2
DAY 1 (MEDIUM)

	Sets	Reps	Rest Period	RM
Front squat/squat jump	3	5	4 minutes	85%
Balance ball push-up/ push-up with clap	3	5	4 minutes	90%
Accelerated step-ups	3	8	3 minutes	90%

DAY 1 (MEDIUM) (continued)

	Sets	Reps	Rest Period
Pull-ups (modified if needed)	3	10+	3 minutes
Balance ball hamstrings	3	12	2 minutes
Alternate leg/arm twisting crunch	3	25+	2 minutes

DAY 2 (HEAVY)

	Sets	Reps	Rest Period	RM
Hang clean	3	6+	3 minutes	70%
Dead lift with hex bar	3	4+	3 minutes	100%
Upper back pull-up from squat rack	3	10+	3 minutes	
Crunches (with weight if able)	3	15+	2 minutes	
Shoulder raises with dumbbell	3	10-8-6	2 minutes	100%
Dips (negative if needed)	3	8+	3 minutes	
Wrist curls	3	12+	2 minutes	

DAY 3 (HEAVY)

	Sets	Reps	Rest Period	RM
One-leg squats to cone touch	3	12	3 minutes	
Push-ups to T stance	3	15+	2 minutes	
Side lunge	3	10	3 minutes	85%
Medicine ball seated crunch twist	3	30+	2 minutes	
Romanian dead lift	3	6+	3 minutes	85%
Balance ball low abs	3	15+	2 minutes	
Rotator cuff	3	15	2 minutes	

WEEK 3
DAY 1 (HEAVY)

	Sets	Reps	Rest Period	RM
Front squat/squat jump	3	5	4 minutes	85%
Balance ball push-up/ push-up with clap	3	5	4 minutes	100%
Accelerated step-ups	3	10-8-8+	3 minutes	100%
Pull-ups (modified if needed)	3	12-10-10+	3 minutes	
Balance ball hamstrings	3	15+	2 minutes	
Alternate leg/arm twisting crunch	3	30-30-25+	2 minutes	

	Sets	Reps	Rest Period	RM
Hang clean	3	6	3 minutes	70%
Dead lift with hex bar	3	4	3 minutes	90%
Upper back pull-up from squat rack	3	10+	3 minutes	
Crunches (with weight if able)	3	15+	2 minutes	
Shoulder raises with dumbbell	3	10-8-6	2 minutes	90%
Dips (negative if needed)	3	10-8-8+	3 minutes	
Wrist curls	3	12	2 minutes	

DAY 3 (MEDIUM)

	Sets	Reps	Rest Period	RM
One-leg squats to cone touch	3	12	3 minutes	
Push-ups to T stance	3	15	2 minutes	
Side lunge	3	10	3 minutes	90%
Medicine ball seated crunch twist	3	30+	2 minutes	
Romanian dead lift	3	6	3 minutes	90%
Balance ball low abs	3	15+	2 minutes	
Rotator cuff	3	15	2 minutes	

WEEK 4
DAY 1 (MEDIUM)

	Sets	Reps	Rest Period	RM
Front squat/squat jump	3	5	4 minutes	85%
Balance ball push-up/ push-up with clap	3	5	4 minutes	95%
Accelerated step-ups	3	8	3 minutes	95%
Pull-ups (modified if needed)	3	12-12-10	3 minutes	
Balance ball hamstrings	3	15	2 minutes	
Alternate leg/arm twisting crunch	3	25+	2 minutes	

DAY 2 (HEAVY)

	Sets	Reps	Rest Period	RM
Hang clean	3	6	3 minutes	75%
Dead lift with hex bar	3	4+	3 minutes	100%
Upper back pull-up from squat rack	3	15-10-10	3 minutes	
Crunches (with weight if able)	3	15+	2 minutes	

DAY 2 (HEAVY)

	Sets	Reps	Rest Period	RM
Shoulder raises with dumbbell	3	10-8-6+	2 minutes	100%
Dips (negative if needed)	3	10-10-8+	3 minutes	
Wrist curls	3	12+	2 minutes	

DAY 3 (MEDIUM)

	Sets	Reps	Rest Period	RM
One-leg squats to cone touch	3	15-15-12	3 minutes	
Push-ups to T stance	3	15+	2 minutes	
Side lunge	3	10	3 minutes	95%
Medicine ball seated crunch twist	3	30+	2 minutes	
Romanian dead lift	3	6	3 minutes	95%
Balance ball low abs	3	15+	2 minutes	
Rotator cuff	3	15	2 minutes	

WEEK 5
DAY 1 (HEAVY)

	Sets	Reps	Rest Period	RM
Front squat/squat jump	3	4	4 minutes	85%
Balance ball push-up/ push-up with clap	3	4	4 minutes	100%
Accelerated step-up	3	6+	3 minutes	100%
Pull-ups (modified if needed)	3	15-15-10+	3 minutes	
Balance ball hamstrings	3	15+	2 minutes	
Alternate leg/arm twisting crunch	3	30-30-25+	2 minutes	

DAY 2 (MEDIUM)

	Sets	Reps	Rest Period	RM
Hang clean	3	6	3 minutes	70%
Dead lift with hex bar	3	4	3 minutes	95%
Upper back pull-up from squat rack	3	15-15-10+	3 minutes	
Crunches (with weight if able)	3	20-20-15+	2 minutes	
Shoulder raises with dumbbell	3	10-8-6	2 minutes	95%
Dips (negative if needed)	3	10	3 minutes	
Wrist curls	3	12	2 minutes	

DAY 3 (HEAVY)

	Sets	Reps	Rest Period	RM
One-leg squats to cone touch	3	15+	3 minutes	
Push-ups to T stance	3	20-15-15+	2 minutes	
Side lunge	3	8+	3 minutes	100%
Medicine ball seated crunch twist	3	30+	2 minutes	
Romanian dead lift	3	6+	3 minutes	100%
Balance ball low abs	3	20-15-15+	2 minutes	
Rotator cuff	3	15	2 minutes	

11

SPORT-SPECIFIC PROGRAMS: VOLLEYBALL

Volleyball players need to possess a unique combination of strength, power, and agility to excel at their sport. The distinct motions involved in jumping, spiking, setting, blocking, and digging involve different muscle actions that are addressed in this program.

The sumo exercises performed with a medicine ball—so named because you start in a position that makes you look like a sumo wrestler—simulate the digging and setting motions, and the wood chopping exercises with the medicine ball develop balance and power in your trunk and upper back that aids you in the spiking motion. Hang cleans or front squats to squat jumps increase your explosiveness so that you can elevate yourself off the floor.

In addition, lunges with a twist to your front leg force you to rotate your trunk, which simulates the motion you make when you reach to hit a ball on either side of you. Push-ups performed using a balance ball work your chest muscles not unlike an incline press, but they also make you concentrate on balance and coordination. They prepare your muscles for motions like setting the ball or blocking the ball with your arms in front of you.

VOLLEYBALL PROGRAM

New exercises

Front squats

Shoulder raises with dumbbell

Push press

112

Pec fly
Power shrug
Incline press
Pullover

Additional equipment
Medicine ball

TRANSITION WEEK

DAY 1 (MEDIUM)

Rest Period: 3 minutes
Repetition Maximum (RM): 85%

	Sets	Reps
Front squats	2	10
Bench press	2	10
Leg curls (hamstrings)	2	10
Lat pulls (close grip)	2	10
Twisting sit-ups	2	20
Shoulder raises with dumbbell	2	12
Crunches	2	20
Biceps curls	2	12
Standing calf	2	12
Triceps	2	12

DAY 2 (MEDIUM)

Rest Period: 3 minutes
Repetition Maximum (RM): 85%

	Sets	Reps
Push press	2	6
Dead lift with hex bar	2	6
Pec fly	2	10
Seated leg curl	2	10
Low row	2	10
Seated calf	2	12
Standing row	2	12
Medicine ball seated twist	2	20
Triceps	2	12
Hip abduction/adduction	2	12
Wrist curls	2	12

DAY 3 (MEDIUM)

Rest Period: 3 minutes
Repetition Maximum (RM): 85%

	Sets	Reps
Dot drill		
Power shrug	2	6
Incline press	2	10
Lat pulls (wide grip)	2	10
Hip abduction/adduction	2	10
Pullover	2	12
Leg extension	2	12
Twisting sit-ups	2	20
Biceps curls	2	12
Crunches	2	20
Wrist curls	2	12

HYPERTROPHY PROGRAM—8 WEEKS

WEEK 1

DAY 1 (MEDIUM)

Rest Period: 3 minutes
Repetition Maximum (RM): 90%

	Sets	Reps
Front squats	3	10
Bench press	3	10
Leg curls (hamstrings)	3	10
Lat pulls (close grip)	3	10
Twisting sit-ups	3	20
Shoulder raises with dumbbell	3	12
Crunches	3	20
Biceps curls	3	12
Standing calf	3	12
Triceps	3	12

DAY 2 (MEDIUM)

Rest Period: 3 minutes
Repetition Maximum (RM): 90%

	Sets	Reps
Push press	3	6
Dead lift with hex bar	3	6
Pec fly	3	10
Seated leg curl	3	10

	Sets	Reps
Low row	3	10
Seated calf	3	12
Standing row	3	12
Medicine ball seated twist	3	20
Triceps	3	12
Hip abduction/adduction	3	12
Wrist curls	3	12

DAY 3 (MEDIUM)

Rest Period: 3 minutes
Repetition Maximum (RM): 90%

	Sets	Reps
Power shrug	3	6
Incline press	3	10
Lat pulls (wide grip)	3	10
Hip abduction/adduction	3	10
Pullover	3	12
Leg extension	3	12
Twisting sit-ups	3	20
Biceps curls	3	12
Crunches	3	20
Wrist curls	3	12

WEEK 2

DAY 1 (HEAVY)

Rest Period: 3 minutes
Repetition Maximum (RM): 100%

	Sets	Reps
Front squats	3	10+
Bench press	3	10+
Leg curls (hamstrings)	3	10+
Lat pulls (close grip)	3	10+
Twisting sit-ups	3	20+
Shoulder raises with dumbbell	3	12+
Crunches	3	20+
Biceps curls	3	12+
Standing calf	3	12+
Triceps	3	12+

DAY 2 (LIGHT)

Rest Period: 3 minutes
Repetition Maximum (RM): 85%

DAY 2 (LIGHT) (continued)

	Sets	Reps
Push press	3	6
Dead lift with hex bar	3	6
Pec fly	3	10
Seated leg curl	3	10
Low row	3	10
Seated calf	3	12
Standing row	3	12
Medicine ball seated twist	3	20
Triceps	3	12
Hip abduction/adduction	3	12
Wrist curls	3	12

DAY 3 (MEDIUM)

Rest Period: 3 minutes
Repetition Maximum (RM): 90%

	Sets	Reps
Power shrug	3	6
Incline press	3	10
Lat pulls (wide grip)	3	10
Hip abduction/adduction	3	10
Pullover	3	12
Leg extension	3	12
Twisting sit-ups	3	20
Biceps curls	3	12
Crunches	3	20
Wrist curls	3	12

WEEK 3

DAY 1 (LIGHT)

Rest Period: variable
Repetition Maximum (RM): 85%

	Sets	Reps	Rest Period
Back squats	3	10	3 minutes
Bench press	3	10	3 minutes
Leg curls (hamstrings)	3	10	3 minutes
Lat pulls (close grip)	3	10	3 minutes
Twisting sit-ups	3	20	2 minutes
Standing rows	3	12	2 minutes
Crunches	3	20	2 minutes
Biceps curls	3	12	2 minutes
Standing calf	3	12	2 minutes
Triceps	3	12	2 minutes

DAY 2 (HEAVY)

Rest Period: variable
Repetition Maximum (RM): 100%

	Sets	Reps	Rest Period
Push press	3	6+	3 minutes
Dead lift with hex bar	3	6+	3 minutes
Pec fly	3	10+	3 minutes
Seated leg curl	3	10+	3 minutes
Low row	3	10+	3 minutes
Seated calf	3	12+	2 minutes
Standing row	3	12+	2 minutes
Medicine ball seated twist	3	20+	2 minutes
Triceps	3	12+	2 minutes
Hip abduction/adduction	3	12+	2 minutes
Wrist curls	3	12+	2 minutes

DAY 3 (MEDIUM)

Rest Period: variable
Repetition Maximum (RM): 95%

	Sets	Reps
Power shrug	3	6
Incline press	3	10
Lat pulls (wide grip)	3	10
Hip abduction/adduction	3	10
Pullover	3	12
Leg extension	3	12
Twisting sit-ups	3	20
Biceps curls	3	12
Crunches	3	20
Wrist curls	3	12

WEEK 4

DAY 1 (HEAVY)

Rest Period: 2 minutes
Repetition Maximum (RM): variable

	Sets	Reps	RM
Front squats	4	10	85%-90%-95%-100%
Bench press	4	10	85%-90%-95%-100%
Leg curls (hamstrings)	3	10+	85%
Lat pulls (close grip)	3	10+	100%
Twisting sit-ups	3	20+	100%
Standing rows	3	12+	100%
Crunches	3	20+	100%
Biceps curls	3	12+	100%

DAY 1 (HEAVY) (continued)

	Sets	Reps	RM
Standing calf	3	12+	100%
Triceps	3	12+	100%

DAY 2 (MEDIUM)
Rest Period: 2 minutes (3 minutes for push press)
Repetition Maximum (RM): 90%

	Sets	Reps
Push press	4	6
Dead lift with hex bar	4	6
Pec fly	3	10
Seated leg curl	3	10
Low row	3	10
Seated calf	3	10
Standing row	3	10
Medicine ball seated twist	3	20
Triceps	3	10
Hip abduction/adduction	3	10
Wrist curls	3	10

DAY 3 (LIGHT)
Rest Period: 2 minutes (3 minutes for power shrug)
Repetition Maximum (RM): 85%

	Sets	Reps
Power shrug	4	6
Incline press	4	10
Lat pulls (wide grip)	4	10
Hip abduction/adduction	3	10
Pullover	3	10
Leg extension	3	10
Twisting sit-ups	3	20
Biceps curls	3	10
Crunches	3	20
Wrist curls	3	10

WEEK 5
DAY 1 (MEDIUM)
Rest Period: variable
Repetition Maximum (RM): 90%

	Sets	Reps	Rest Period
Back squats	4	10	2 minutes
Bench press	4	10	2 minutes

	Sets	Reps	Rest Period
Leg curls (hamstrings)	3	10	1 minute
Lat pulls (close grip)	3	10	2 minutes
Twisting sit-ups	3	20	1 minute
Standing rows	3	10	2 minutes
Crunches	3	20	1 minute
Biceps curls	3	10	1 minute
Standing calf	3	10	1 minute
Triceps	3	10	1 minute

DAY 2 (MEDIUM)

Rest Period: variable
Repetition Maximum (RM): 90%

	Sets	Reps	Rest Period
Push press	4	6	3 minutes
Dead lift with hex bar	4	6	2 minutes
Pec fly	3	10	2 minutes
Seated leg curl	3	10	2 minutes
Low row	3	10	2 minutes
Seated calf	3	10	1 minute
Standing row	3	10	1 minute
Medicine ball seated twist	3	20	1 minute
Triceps	3	10	1 minute
Hip abduction/ adduction	3	10	1 minute
Wrist curls	3	10	1 minute

DAY 3 (HEAVY)

Rest Period: variable
Repetition Maximum (RM): variable

	Sets	Reps	Rest Period	RM
Power shrug	4	6	3 minutes	85%-90%-95%-100%
Incline press	4	10	2 minutes	85%-90%-95%-100%
Lat pulls (wide grip)	4	10+	2 minutes	100%
Hip abduction/ adduction	3	10+	1 minute	100%
Pullover	3	10+	1 minute	100%
Leg extension	3	10+	1 minute	100%
Twisting sit-ups	3	20+	1 minute	100%
Biceps curls	3	10+	1 minute	100%
Crunches	3	20+	1 minute	100%
Wrist curls	3	10+	1 minute	100%

WEEK 6
DAY 1 (MEDIUM)

Rest Period: 1 minute
Repetition Maximum (RM): 90%

	Sets	Reps
Back squats	4	10
Bench press	4	10
Lat pulls (close grip)	3	10
Leg curls (hamstrings)	3	10
Standing calf	3	10
Twisting sit-ups	3	20
Standing rows	3	10
Crunches	3	20
Biceps curls	3	10
Triceps	3	10

DAY 2 (HEAVY)

Rest Period: variable
Repetition Maximum (RM): variable

	Sets	Reps	Rest Period	RM
Push press	4	6	3 minutes	85%-90%-95%-100%
Dead lift with hex bar	4	6	2 minutes	85%-90%-95%-100%
Pec fly	3	10	1 minute	100%
Seated leg curl	3	10	1 minute	100%
Low row	4	10	2 minutes	85%-90%-95%-100%
Seated calf	3	10+	1 minute	100%
Shoulder raises with dumbbell	3	10+	1 minute	100%
Medicine ball seated twist	3	20+	1 minute	100%
Triceps	3	10+	1 minute	100%
Hip abduction/adduction	3	10+	1 minute	100%
Wrist curls	3	10+	1 minute	100%

DAY 3 (MEDIUM)

Rest Period: 1 minute (3 minutes for power shrug)
Repetition Maximum (RM): 90%

	Sets	Reps
Power shrug	4	6
Incline press	4	10
Lat pulls (wide grip)	4	10

	Sets	Reps
Hip abduction/adduction	3	10
Pullover	3	10
Leg extension	3	10
Twisting sit-ups	3	20
Biceps curls	3	10
Crunches	3	20
Wrist curls	3	10

WEEK 7
DAY 1 (HEAVY)

Rest Period: variable
Repetition Maximum (RM): variable

	Sets	Reps	Rest Period	RM
Back squats	4	10	2 minutes	85%-90%-95%-100%
Bench press	4	10	2 minutes	85%-90%-95%-100%
Lat pulls (close grip)	3	10+	1 minute	100%
Leg curls (hamstrings)	4	10	1 minute	100%
Standing calf	3	10+	1 minute	100%
Twisting sit-ups	4	20-20-20-10+	1 minute	
Standing row	3	10+	1 minute	100%
Crunches	3	10+	1 minute	
Biceps curls	3	10+	1 minute	100%
Back extension	3	20+	1 minute	100%
Triceps	3	10+	1 minute	100%

DAY 2 (MEDIUM)

Rest Period: 1 minute (3 minutes for push press)
Repetition Maximum (RM): 90%

	Sets	Reps
Push press	4	6
Dead lift with hex bar	4	10
Pec fly	4	10
Low row	4	10
Shoulder raises with dumbbell	3	10
Seated leg curl	3	10
Hip abduction/adduction	3	10
Seated calf	3	10
Medicine ball seated twist	3	20

DAY 2 (MEDIUM) (continued)

	Sets	Reps
Triceps	3	10
Wrist curls	3	10

DAY 3 (HEAVY)

Rest Period: variable
Repetition Maximum (RM): variable

	Sets	Reps	Rest Period	RM
Power shrug	4	6	3 minutes	85%-90%-95%-100%
Incline press	4	10	2 minutes	85%-90%-95%-100%
Lat pulls (wide grip)	4	10	2 minutes	85%-90%-95%-100%
Pullover	3	10+	1 minute	
Hip abduction/ adduction	4	10-10-10-12	1 minute	85%-90%-95%-100%
Leg extension	3	10+	1 minute	
Twisting sit-ups	3	20+	1 minute	
Biceps curls	3	10+	1 minute	
Crunches	3	20+	1 minute	
Good morning	3	10+	1 minute	

WEEK 8

DAY 1 (MEDIUM)

Rest Period: 1 minute
Repetition Maximum (RM): 90%

	Sets	Reps
Back squats	3	10
Bench press	3	10
Lat pulls (close grip)	3	10
Leg curls (hamstrings)	3	10
Standing calf	3	10
Twisting sit-ups	3	20
Standing row	3	10
Crunches	3	10
Biceps curls	3	10
Back extension	3	20
Triceps	3	10

DAY 2 (MEDIUM)

Rest Period: 1 minute (3 minutes for push press)
Repetition Maximum (RM): 90%

	Sets	Reps
Push press	3	6
Dead lift with hex bar	3	10
Pec fly	3	10
Low row	3	10
Shoulder raises with dumbbell	3	10
Seated leg curl	3	10
Hip abduction/adduction	3	10
Seated calf	3	10
Medicine ball seated twist	3	20
Triceps	3	10
Wrist curls	3	10

DAY 3 (MEDIUM)

Rest Period: 1 minute (3 minutes for power shrug)
Repetition Maximum (RM): 85%

	Sets	Reps
Power shrug	3	6
Incline press	3	10
Lat pulls (wide grip)	3	10
Pullover	3	10
Hip abduction/adduction	3	10
Leg extension	3	10
Twisting sit-ups	3	20
Biceps curls	3	10
Crunches	3	20
Good morning	3	10

STRENGTH PROGRAM—6 WEEKS

New exercises

Balance ball incline press with dumbbell

Hang clean

Side lunge

Medicine ball wood chops

Medicine ball sumo squats

Medicine ball sit-up and twist

Medicine ball lunge with twist to front leg

Balance ball hamstrings

Additional equipment

Medicine ball

Balance ball

Parallel bars

Chin-up bar

WEEK 1
DAY 1 (MEDIUM)

Rest Period: 3
Repetition Maximum (RM): 90%

	Sets	Reps
Hang clean	3	6
Back squats	3	8
Balance ball incline press with dumbbell	3	8
Romanian dead lift	3	8
Leg curl (hamstrings)	3	8
Single rows with dumbbell	3	8
Side lunge	3	8
Twisting sit-ups	3	25+
Standing calf	3	8
Medicine ball sumo swing to eye height	3	12

DAY 2 (MEDIUM)

Rest Period: 3 minutes
Repetition Maximum (RM): 90%

	Sets	Reps
Push press	3	6
Medicine ball sumo squats	3	12
Medicine ball sit-up and twist	3	20+
Pull-ups (modified if needed)	3	8
Balance ball low abs	3	10+
Low row	3	8
Shoulder raises with dumbbell	3	10
Dips (negative if needed)	3	8
Biceps curls	3	10
Wrist curls	3	10

DAY 3 (MEDIUM)

Rest Period: 3 minutes
Repetition Maximum (RM): 90%

	Sets	Reps
High pull	3	6
Bench press	3	10
Medicine ball lunge with twist to front leg	3	10
Twisting sit-ups	3	25+
Balance ball hamstrings	3	10
Step-ups	3	10
Plyometric sit-ups (low abs)	3	10+
Pullover	3	10
Rotator cuff	3	15

WEEK 2

DAY 1 (MEDIUM)

Rest Period: 3 minutes
Repetition Maximum (RM): 90%

	Sets	Reps
Hang clean	4	6
Back squats	4	8
Balance ball incline press with dumbbell	4	8
Romanian dead lift	4	8
Leg curl (hamstrings)	4	8
Single rows with dumbbell	4	8
Side lunge	4	8
Twisting sit-ups	4	25+
Standing calf	4	8
Medicine ball sumo swing to eye height	4	12

DAY 2 (LIGHT)

Rest Period: 3 minutes
Repetition Maximum (RM): 85%

	Sets	Reps
Push press (last set with wooden dowel)	4	6-6-6-25
Medicine ball sumo squats	4	12
Medicine ball sit-up and twist	4	6
Pull-ups (modified if needed)	4	20+
Balance ball low abs	4	8
Low row	4	8
Shoulder raises with dumbbell	4	8
Dips (negative if needed)	4	10

DAY 2 (LIGHT) (continued)

	Sets	Reps
Biceps curls	4	8
Wrist curls	4	10

DAY 3 (MEDIUM)

Rest Period: 3 minutes
Repetition Maximum (RM): 90%

	Sets	Reps
High pull	4	6
Bench press	4	10
Medicine ball lunge with twist to front leg	4	10
Twisting sit-ups	4	25+
Balance ball hamstrings	4	10
Step-ups	4	10
Plyometric sit-ups (low abs)	4	10+
Pullover	4	10
Rotator cuff	4	15

WEEK 3

DAY 1 (MEDIUM)

Rest Period: variable
Repetition Maximum (RM): 95%

	Sets	Reps	Rest Period
Hang clean	4	6	3 minutes
Back squats	4	8	3 minutes
Balance ball incline press with dumbbell	4	8	3 minutes
Romanian dead lift	4	8	2 minutes
Leg curl (hamstrings)	4	8	2 minutes
Single rows with dumbbell	4	8	3 minutes
Side lunge	4	8	2 minutes
Twisting sit-ups	4	25+	3 minutes
Standing calf	4	8	3 minutes
Medicine ball sumo swing to eye height	4	12	3 minutes

DAY 2 (HEAVY)

Rest Period: variable
Repetition Maximum (RM): variable

	Sets	Reps	Rest Period	RM
Push press	4	6	3 minutes	85%-90%-95%-100%

	Sets	Reps	Rest Period	RM
Medicine ball sumo squats	4	12	3 minutes	
Medicine ball sit-up and twist	4	25-20-20-20+	2 minutes	
Pull-ups (modified if needed)	4	8+	2 minutes	
Balance ball low abs	4	8+	3 minutes	
Low row	4	8+	2 minutes	100%
Shoulder raises with dumbbell	4	8+	2 minutes	100%
Dips (negative if needed)	4	10+	2 minutes	
Biceps curls	4	8+	2 minutes	100%
Wrist curls	4	10+	2 minutes	100%

DAY 3 (LIGHT)

Rest Period: variable
Repetition Maximum (RM): 85%

	Sets	Reps	Rest Period
High pull	4	6-6-6-25	3 minutes
Bench press	4	6	3 minutes
Medicine ball lunge with twist to front leg	4	10	3 minutes
Twisting sit-ups	4	25+	3 minutes
Balance ball hamstrings	4	8	2 minutes
Step-ups	4	8	2 minutes
Plyometric sit-ups (low abs)	4	10	2 minutes
Pullover	4	10	2 minutes
Rotator cuff	4	10	2 minutes

WEEK 4
DAY 1 (MEDIUM)

Rest Period: variable
Repetition Maximum (RM): 90%

	Sets	Reps	Rest Period
Hang clean	4	6	3 minutes
Back squats	4	10-8-6-4	3 minutes
Balance ball incline press with dumbbell	4	10-8-6-4	2 minutes
Romanian dead lift	4	10-8-6-4	2 minutes
Leg curl (hamstrings)	4	10-8-6-4	2 minutes
Single rows with dumbbell	4	10-8-6-4	2 minutes
Side lunge	4	10-8-6-4	2 minutes
Twisting sit-ups	4	30-25-25-25+	2 minutes
Standing calf	4	10-8-6-4	2 minutes

DAY 1 (MEDIUM) (continued)

	Sets	Reps	Rest Period
Medicine ball sumo swing to eye height	4	15-15-12-12	2 minutes

DAY 2 (MEDIUM)

Rest Period: 2 minutes (3 minutes for dead lift)
Repetition Maximum (RM): 90%

	Sets	Reps
Medicine ball sumo squats	4	15-12-12-12
Dead lift with hex bar	4	6-5-4-3
Medicine ball sit-up and twist	3	25-25-20
Pull-ups (modified if needed)	3	10
Balance ball low abs	4	10
Low row	4	10-8-6-4
Shoulder raises with dumbbell	4	10-8-6-4
Dips (negative if needed)	3	10
Biceps curls	3	10-8-6
Wrist curls	3	10

DAY 3 (HEAVY)

Rest Period: 2 minutes (3 minutes for high pull)
Repetition Maximum (RM): 100%

	Sets	Reps
High pull	4	6-5-4-2+
Bench press	4	6+
Medicine ball lunge with twist to front leg	4	10+
Twisting sit-ups	4	30-30-25-25+
Balance ball hamstrings	3	8+
Step-ups	3	10-8-6+
Plyometric sit-ups (low abs)	3	15-15-10+
Pullover	3	10+
Rotator cuff	3	10

WEEK 5

DAY 1 (HEAVY)

Rest Period: variable
Repetition Maximum (RM): 100%

	Sets	Reps	Rest Period
Hang clean	3	6+	3 minutes
Back squats	3	7+	3 minutes
Balance ball incline press with dumbbell	3	7+	2 minutes

	Sets	Reps	Rest Period
Romanian dead lift	3	7+	2 minutes
Leg curl (hamstrings)	3	7+	2 minutes
Single rows with dumbbell	3	7+	2 minutes
Side lunge	3	7+	2 minutes
Twisting sit-ups	3	30-25-25+	2 minutes
Standing calf	3	7+	2 minutes
Medicine ball sumo swing to eye height	3	15-15-12+	2 minutes

DAY 2 (MEDIUM)

Rest Period: 2 minutes (3 minutes for dead lift)
Repetition Maximum (RM): 95%

	Sets	Reps
Medicine ball sumo squats	3	15-15-12
Dead lift with hex bar	3	6
Medicine ball sit-up and twist	3	25
Pull-ups (modified if needed)	3	12
Balance ball low abs	3	12
Low row	3	7
Shoulder raises with dumbbell	3	8
Dips (negative if needed)	3	12
Biceps curls	3	8
Wrist curls	3	10

DAY 3 (MEDIUM)

Rest Period: variable
Repetition Maximum (RM): 90%

	Sets	Reps	Rest Period
High pull	3	6	3 minutes
Bench press	3	6	3 minutes
Medicine ball lunge with twist to front leg	3	10	3 minutes
Twisting sit-ups	3	30+	3 minutes
Balance ball hamstrings	3	10+	2 minutes
Step-ups	3	8	2 minutes
Plyometric sit-ups (low abs)	3	25	2 minutes
Pullover	3	10	2 minutes
Rotator cuff	3	10	2 minutes

WEEK 6
DAY 1 (LIGHT)

Rest Period: 2 minutes (3 minutes for hang clean)
Repetition Maximum (RM): 85%

DAY 1 (LIGHT) (continued)

	Sets	Reps
Hang clean	3	6
Back squats	3	6
Balance ball incline press with dumbbell	3	6
Romanian dead lift	3	6
Leg curl (hamstrings)	3	8
Single rows with dumbbell	3	6
Side lunge	3	8
Twisting sit-ups	3	30
Standing calf	3	8
Medicine ball sumo swing to eye height	3	15

DAY 2 (MEDIUM)

Rest Period: variable
Repetition Maximum (RM): 90%

	Sets	Reps	Rest Period
Medicine ball sumo squats	3	15	2 minutes
Dead lift with hex bar	3	6	3 minutes
Medicine ball sit-up and twist	3	30-30-25	2 minutes
Pull-ups (modified if needed)	3	12+	2 minutes
Balance ball low abs	3	12+	3 minutes
Low row	3	8	3 minutes
Shoulder raises with dumbbell	3	25-20-20	2 minutes
Dips (negative if needed)	3	12-12-10+	2 minutes
Biceps curls	3	8	2 minutes
Wrist curls	3	10	2 minutes

DAY 3 (HEAVY)

Rest Period: variable
Repetition Maximum (RM): variable

	Sets	Reps	Rest Period	RM
High pull	3	6	3 minutes	90%-95%-100%
Bench press	3	6+	3 minutes	90%-95%-100%
Medicine ball lunge with twist to front leg	3	8+	3 minutes	100%
Twisting sit-ups	3	35-30-30+	3 minutes	
Balance ball hamstrings	3	10+	2 minutes	100%
Step-ups	3	8+	2 minutes	
Plyometric sit-ups (low abs)	3	25	2 minutes	
Pullover	3	10	2 minutes	100%
Rotator cuff	3	10	2 minutes	100%

POWER PROGRAM—5 WEEKS

New exercises

Front squat to squat jump

Dumbbell bench press to push-up with clap

Accelerated step-up

Alternate leg/arm twisting crunch

Hang clean to push press

Medicine ball sumo swing to eye height

Upper back pull-up from squat rack

One-leg squats to toe raise

Push-ups on balance ball

Additional equipment

Medicine ball

Chin-up bar

Step-up box

Balance ball

Parallel bars

WEEK 1
DAY 1 (LIGHT)

	Sets	Reps	Rest Period	RM
Front squat/squat jump	3	5	4 minutes	85%
Bench press with dumbbell/ push-up with clap	3	5	4 minutes	85%
Accelerated step-up	3	8	3 minutes	85%
Pull-ups (modified if needed)	3	10	3 minutes	
Balance ball hamstrings	3	12	2 minutes	
Alternate leg/arm twisting crunch	3	25+	2 minutes	

DAY 2 (MEDIUM)

	Sets	Reps	Rest Period	RM
Hang clean to push press	3	6	3 minutes	70%
Medicine ball sumo swing to eye height	3	12	3 minutes	
Upper back pull-up from squat rack	3	10	3 minutes	

DAY 2 (MEDIUM) (continued)

	Sets	Reps	Rest Period	RM
Crunches (with weight if able)	3	15+	2 minutes	
Shoulder raises with dumbbell	3	10-8-6	2 minutes	95%
Dips (negative if needed)	3	8	3 minutes	
Wrist curls	3	12	2 minutes	

DAY 3 (HEAVY)

	Sets	Reps	Rest Period	RM
One-leg squats to toe raise	3	12	3 minutes	
Push-ups on balance ball	3	15+	2 minutes	
Side lunge	3	10+	3 minutes	100%
Medicine ball seated crunch twist	3	30+	2 minutes	
Romanian dead lift	3	6+	3 minutes	100%
Balance ball low abs	3	15+	2 minutes	
Rotator cuff	3	15	2 minutes	

WEEK 2

DAY 1 (MEDIUM)

	Sets	Reps	Rest Period	RM
Front squat/squat jump	3	5	4 minutes	85%
Bench press with dumbbell/ push-up with clap	3	5	4 minutes	85%
Accelerated step-up	3	8	3 minutes	90%
Pull-ups (modified if needed)	3	10+	3 minutes	
Balance ball hamstrings	3	12	2 minutes	
Alternate leg/arm twisting crunch	3	25+	2 minutes	

DAY 2 (HEAVY)

	Sets	Reps	Rest Period	RM
Hang clean to push press	3	6+	3 minutes	70%
Medicine ball sumo swing to eye height	3	12+	3 minutes	
Upper back pull-up from squat rack	3	10+	3 minutes	
Crunches (with weight if able)	3	15+	2 minutes	
Shoulder raises with dumbbell	3	10-8-6+	2 minutes	100%

	Sets	Reps	Rest Period	RM
Dips (negative if needed)	3	8+	3 minutes	
Wrist curls	3	12+	2 minutes	

DAY 3 (LIGHT)

	Sets	Reps	Rest Period	RM
One-leg squats to toe raise	3	12	3 minutes	
Push-ups on balance ball	3	15+	2 minutes	
Side lunge	3	10	3 minutes	85%
Medicine ball seated crunch twist	3	30+	2 minutes	
Romanian dead lift	3	6+	3 minutes	85%
Balance ball low abs	3	15+	2 minutes	
Rotator cuff	3	15	2 minutes	

WEEK 3
DAY 1 (HEAVY)

	Sets	Reps	Rest Period	RM
Front squat/squat jump	3	5	4 minutes	85%
Bench press with dumbbell/				
push-up with clap	3	5	4 minutes	85%
Accelerated step-up	3	8+	3 minutes	100%
Pull-ups (modified if needed)	3	10+	3 minutes	
Balance ball hamstrings	3	15+	2 minutes	
Alternate leg/arm twisting crunch	3	25+	2 minutes	

DAY 2 (MEDIUM)

	Sets	Reps	Rest Period	RM
Hang clean to push press	3	6	3 minutes	70%
Medicine ball sumo swing				
to eye height	3	14-14-12	3 minutes	
Upper back pull-up from				
squat rack	3	10+	3 minutes	
Crunches (with weight if able)	3	15+	2 minutes	
Shoulder raises with dumbbell	3	10-8-6	2 minutes	90%
Dips (negative if needed)	3	10-8-8+	3 minutes	
Wrist curls	3	12	2 minutes	

DAY 3 (MEDIUM)

	Sets	Reps	Rest Period	RM
One-leg squats to toe raise	3	12	3 minutes	
Push-ups on balance ball	3	15	2 minutes	
Side lunge	3	10	3 minutes	90%
Medicine ball seated crunch				
twist	3	30+	2 minutes	

DAY 3 (MEDIUM) (continued)

	Sets	Reps	Rest Period	RM
Romanian dead lift	3	6	3 minutes	90%
Balance ball low abs	3	15+	2 minutes	
Rotator cuff	3	15	2 minutes	

WEEK 4
DAY 1 (MEDIUM)

	Sets	Reps	Rest Period	RM
Front squat/squat jump	3	5	4 minutes	85%
Bench press with dumbbell/ push-up with clap	3	5	4 minutes	85%
Accelerated step-up	3	8	3 minutes	95%
Pull-ups (modified if needed)	3	12-12-10	3 minutes	
Balance ball hamstrings	3	15	2 minutes	
Alternate leg/arm twisting crunch	3	25+	2 minutes	

DAY 2 (HEAVY)

	Sets	Reps	Rest Period	RM
Hang clean to push press	3	6	3 minutes	75%
Medicine ball sumo swing to eye height	3	14-14-12+	3 minutes	
Upper back pull-up from squat rack	3	15-10-10+	3 minutes	
Crunches (with weight if able)	3	15+	2 minutes	
Shoulder raises with dumbbell	3	10-8-6+	2 minutes	100%
Dips (negative if needed)	3	10-10-8+	3 minutes	
Wrist curls	3	12+	2 minutes	

DAY 3 (MEDIUM)

	Sets	Reps	Rest Period	RM
One-leg squats to toe raise	3	15-15-12+	3 minutes	
Push-ups on balance ball	3	15+	2 minutes	
Side lunge	3	10	3 minutes	95%
Medicine ball seated crunch twist	3	30+	2 minutes	
Romanian dead lift	3	6	3 minutes	95%
Balance ball low abs	3	15+	2 minutes	
Rotator cuff	3	15	2 minutes	

WEEK 5
DAY 1 (HEAVY)

	Sets	Reps	Rest Period	RM
Front squat/squat jump	3	4	4 minutes	85%
Bench press with dumbbell/ **push-up with clap**	3	4	4 minutes	85%
Accelerated step-up	3	6+	3 minutes	85%
Pull-ups (modified if needed)	3	15-15-10+	3 minutes	
Balance ball hamstrings	3	15+	2 minutes	
Alternate leg/arm twisting crunch	3	30-30-25+	2 minutes	

DAY 2 (MEDIUM)

	Sets	Reps	Rest Period	RM
Hang clean to push press	3	6	3 minutes	70%
Medicine ball sumo swing to eye height	3	14	3 minutes	
Upper back pull-up from squat rack	3	15-15-10+	3 minutes	
Crunches (with weight if able)	3	20-20-15+	2 minutes	
Shoulder raises with dumbbell	3	10-8-6	2 minutes	95%
Dips (negative if needed)	3	10	3 minutes	
Wrist curls	3	12	2 minutes	

DAY 3 (HEAVY)

	Sets	Reps	Rest Period	RM
One-leg squats to toe raise	3	15+	3 minutes	
Push-ups on balance ball	3	20-15-15+	2 minutes	
Side lunge	3	8+	3 minutes	100%
Medicine ball seated crunch twist	3	30+	2 minutes	
Romanian dead lift	3	6+	3 minutes	100%
Balance ball low abs	3	15+	2 minutes	
Rotator cuff	3	15	2 minutes	

12

NUTRITION

THE BASICS

Everyone needs to eat right, but especially athletes who are pushing their bodies to the limits of fatigue and endurance and need to replace depleted stores of energy. Some athletes use supplements and other products to enhance their training. These will be addressed later in this chapter, but it is important to remember that a healthy, balanced diet and a good plan are more than sufficient to keep you fit and performing at your best. A healthy diet for an athlete is also a healthy basic diet—the proper balance of protein, fat, and carbohydrates.

Understanding what foods you need in your diet requires an understanding of the elements contained in those foods and what they do for you:

Proteins

Tissues in your body need proteins to grow and to heal. Proteins supply amino acids, assist in the formation of hormones and enzymes, and aid the development of antibodies. Most Americans eat more protein than they need. The general recommendation is to get 20–30 percent of your daily calories from protein. It is important to eat it every day.

Water

Your body is made up largely of water, and your body needs a lot of water every day. Water helps to maintain body temperature, lubricate and cushion organs, transport nutrients, and flush toxins from the body. Water also regulates your temperament. If you are dehydrated, not only will you get fatigued and irritable, you may be inviting more serious illnesses.

Carbohydrates

When your body digests foods, it breaks them down into substances that it can use. Carbohydrates become glucose molecules which the body can use easily and efficiently. Glucose enters the bloodstream and feeds muscles, organs, and the brain.

There are two types of carbohydrates: simple and complex. Simple carbohydrates do not, by themselves, offer your body much in the way of nutritional value. They include refined sugars (like white sugar) and sugars that occur naturally (like those found in fruit). Complex carbohydrates are also known as starches and fibers. They occur in breads, pasta, fruits, and vegetables, and are very valuable to your body.

Fats

Too much fat can contribute to obesity, heart disease, and cancer. But fat also plays a vital nutritional role. Fats can insulate your body, protect nerve pathways and organs, and provide vehicles for fat-soluble vitamins. They also give your body a sense of fullness, which can prevent overeating.

So, you need fat in your diet, but you need to be careful. You want to make sure you are eating the right kind of fat, and the right amount.

KINDS OF FAT
When you think of fat, realize that it can be saturated or unsaturated. Saturated fats are dangerous. They can squeeze into tiny spaces (like an artery), and cause blockages. Saturated fats are solid at room temperature (think of a piece of lard).

Unsaturated fats do not pack together so easily, and thus are less able to cause blockages. The best fats come from vegetable sources (for example, olives, peanuts, and walnuts). These are mono- or polyunsaturated, and are liquids.

AMOUNT OF FAT
Recommendations about the percentage of fat calories in a daily diet vary from 20–30 percent. It's safe to aim for roughly 25–30 percent. (The average American gets 37 percent of calories from fat). In general, aim for moderation, and for the healthiest forms of fat.

Vitamins

Vitamins regulate biochemical reactions in your body. While they do not supply any energy by themselves, they do assist your body in digesting and using nutrients from other sources.

Vitamins can be either fat-soluble or water-soluble. The body stores those which are fat-soluble, so you can build up too many of them if you take them in large quantities. (These include A, D, E, and K). When you take too much of a water-soluble vitamin, your body simply flushes out the excess in urine. A good daily vitamin pill from your pharmacy can supplement the vitamins that your meals may not supply.

Minerals

Minerals perform vital functions in your body. They help carry nerve signals, build bones, and clot blood. Most people do not need mineral supplements.

BALANCE AND MODERATION

If you are training intensively or engaged in in-season competition, you will be expending more energy and thus require more nutrients for refueling. This should not be an excuse to overeat, however. The amount of food you eat should reflect the amount of energy you expend. When you achieve that balance, it is easy to maintain your weight at a healthy level.

Here are some tips:

- Keep your portions modest. When you have a smaller amount of food on your plate, you will find it easier to eat in moderation.
- As much as possible, eat at regular times each day. It is not a good idea to skip meals or to eat too much between meals. When you skip meals, you can get extremely hungry, which can lead to gorging.
- Eat plenty of vegetables, fruits, and grain products. Most of us do not eat enough of these foods. Make an extra effort to keep fresh fruits and vegetables in the house, and to reach for them when you want a snack.
- Avoid eating a lot of fried foods, creamy sauces, butter, red meat, and other high-fat foods. Try to eat skim or low-fat dairy products and lean cuts of meat instead. On the other hand, do not deny yourself all your favorite foods. The key is moderation: eat them in small portions, and relatively infrequently.

- Eat sugar in moderation, and eat moderate amounts of salt and sodium. If you drink alcoholic beverages, do so in moderation.
- Eat a variety of foods that are high in fiber. Fiber plays a critical role in your health. Try to keep it in mind when making food choices: eat fruits with the skins on, and choose whole-grain breads and cereals.
- Drink a lot of water. Every adult needs at least eight 8-ounce glasses of water a day. If you are active, add to that accordingly.

NUTRITION FOR ATHLETES

It is important to remember that athletes can require more protein than sedentary adults. If you exercise strenuously three or more times per week, you should strive for a daily diet that consists of the following ratios:

(To calculate your weight in kilograms, divide your body weight in pounds by 2.2.)

- Carbohydrates: 6 to 8 grams per kilogram of body weight, or about 50–70 percent of total calories
- Protein: 1.6–2.4 grams per kilogram, or about 15–20 percent of total calories
- Fat: 20–30 percent of total calories, and no less than 20 grams per day.

This means a 150-pound athlete's diet should include approximately 409 grams of carbohydrates and 109 grams of protein. Since most protein is high in fat and low in fiber, caution should be used when following a high-protein diet. High-protein diets can cause dehydration and, in extreme cases, kidney disease.

The following foods are good sources of protein:

- Meat, chicken, and fish: about 7 grams per ounce
- Dairy products: about 8–9 grams per cup
- Beans and legumes: about 6–8 grams per half cup.

Fat is a necessary nutrient in the body, but a high-fat diet will increase your risk of heart disease. An athlete's diet should include about 20–30 percent of calories from fat. Though the total number of grams you consume will depend on your calorie intake, you should never go below 20 grams of fat per day. Try to avoid saturated fats from foods such as butter, lard, egg yolks, and red meat, as well as whole-fat dairy products.

Refueling During Your Workout

While you are exercising, you should consume about 25–50 grams of carbohydrates and about 100–200 calories per hour to maintain your energy level. For example, a 16-ounce sports drink typically contains 28 grams of carbohydrates and 100 calories, and an energy bar may contain about 45 grams of carbohydrates.

For refueling, you should try to consume 1–1.5 grams per kilogram of carbohydrates within the first 30 minutes, and approximately 100 grams per hour for two to four hours after you finish your exercise. For example, a 150-pound (68.2 kilograms) athlete should consume between 68 and 102 grams of carbohydrates within 30 minutes.

Here is the carbohydrate content, in grams per serving, of some common foods:

- Bagel: 58
- Baked potato: 50
- Soft pretzel: 38
- Apple: 32
- Banana: 27
- Oatmeal: 27
- Bread (one slice): 11

The best carbohydrates for refueling are those that have a high glycemic index, which is a number that refers to how quickly a food is converted to glucose in the bloodstream. The higher the number, the faster the food will be converted into glucose, which will bring blood-sugar levels back to normal more quickly.

Here are some examples of foods with a high glycemic index, with pure glucose being 100:

- Sport drink (8 oz.): 91
- Baked potato: 85
- Bagel: 72
- Bread (one slice): 71
- Oatmeal or oat cereal (one cup): 61

You will burn more calories and deplete your store of glycogen the longer you work out, so you should replenish your glycogen stores within 30 minutes of ending a workout by consuming 1–1.5 grams of carbohydrate per kilogram of body weight. The average exerciser will not seriously deplete stored glycogen, but it is a good habit to practice carbohydrate refueling after exercise.

Many athletes may feel extra hunger after a workout and overeat. Some fruit juice or a carbohydrate snack immediately after a workout can ease this common urge.

Sports drinks are usually necessary only if you are going to be involved in an activity lasting more than 90 minutes. The best choices are those that contain a 5 percent carbohydrate solution. To get the carbohydrate content of a product, take the total grams of carbohydrates and divide by the total calories per serving.

Products containing high-fructose corn syrup can cause cramping, and should be avoided.

Pre-Workout Meals

Eating a proper pre-workout meal can help give you the maximum amount of energy while easing indigestion, cramps, and stomach pain. Whether you are in school or out, one of the most important things to remember is to be smart about what, when, and how much you eat. Busy schedules do not make this easy, so you may have to do a little planning ahead. Also, you may do your workouts at different times of the day or evening, which makes it doubly important to stay on top of this. Regardless of your schedule, eating too much or too little before a workout can leave you feeling weak or nauseous afterwards.

The best pre-workout meals are balanced, including carbohydrates, protein, and a small amount of fat. You want to make sure your meal has been digested before you begin working out. Greasy fried foods that are heavy in fat take a long time to digest and can cause nausea if eaten before a workout.

A good example of a pre-workout meal is a turkey sandwich, a side salad, and a piece of fruit. The turkey sandwich has protein and carbohydrate, the salad has minerals and roughage to help you digest, and the fruit provides sugar and carbohydrate for added energy. Keep yourself hydrated by accompanying your pre-workout meal with eight to 24 ounces of caffeine-free liquid. To ensure proper digestion, it makes sense to eat three to four hours before your workout. If you are planning a 5:00 workout, eating lunch at 1:00 would be right on target. You would be able to digest your food, avoid stomachaches, and have the optimal amount of sugars available for energy. If you eat lunch at 12:00, you might consider eating a carbohydrate snack right before you work out to provide extra energy.

For longer workouts, you may want to eat about four grams of carbohydrate per kilogram of body weight. (Divide your weight in pounds by 2.2 to determine your weight in kilograms.) You should also drink plenty of fluids throughout the day before your workout.

In general, try to drink eight to 24 ounces of fluid about an hour before a workout. If you have not had a meal in the last four hours prior to a workout, eating a piece of fruit or some crackers, or drinking eight ounces of 100 percent fruit juice can help give you the extra energy you need to push yourself through an effective workout. Depending on the sensitivity of your stomach, you should eat your carbohydrate snack about an hour before a workout.

Some professional athletes use carbohydrate-and-protein supplements that are mixed with liquid for rapid absorption into the muscles. In contrast, eating a bagel or muffin right before a workout causes blood flow to go to the stomach rather than to the muscles for performance.

Finally, keep in mind that, as with your training program, consistency is the key. If your overall diet is lacking in some areas and overemphasizing others, eating the right foods before you work out is not going to turn things around by itself. You should strive for variety, balance, and moderation as a matter of course, whether you are in the middle of an intense stretch of training or taking a breather after a long season.

SUPPLEMENTS

Striving to be the best is a trait shared by athletes at all levels, from beginners to Olympic champions. Unfortunately, the desire to gain an edge on the competition has led to an explosion in the number of nutritional supplements that claim to improve athletic performance. Legislation has allowed manufacturers of these supplements to make claims, mostly unproved, about the effects of their products, as long as they do not claim to treat or cure a specific disease. The result is that the marketplace has become overloaded with products that are harmless at best and contain the potential for harm if they are abused or taken by people who should not be taking them.

First, it is important to differentiate between a drug and a supplement. The former is a substance that has been approved by the Food and Drug Administration (FDA) as having a specific effect on the body, whether to change the body's structure or function or to treat disease. Dietary supplements, on the other hand, do not have to be FDA approved since they are not classified as drugs, and may or may not have any nutritional value at all.

The lack of credible scientific evidence of the benefits for athletes of taking dietary supplements only supports the universally accepted idea that a well-balanced diet that addresses the need for appropriate levels of protein, fats, and carbohydrates will help you meet your athletic goals.

Iron and Calcium

Iron and calcium deficiencies are common among women, and should be addressed if you are embarking on a weight-training program. Low levels of iron can lead to fatigue and decreased performance, or to a low blood count, a condition known as anemia. To avoid this, eat foods that are rich in iron such as meat, chicken, or fish. At the same time, make sure to consume citrus fruits and juices, as citrus aids your body's absorption of iron. Do not take iron supplements without consulting your physician, since too much iron can be dangerous to your health.

Many women do not consume enough calcium on a daily basis. This can be exacerbated by intense training, which can lead to irregular menstrual cycles and in turn to decreased bone density. This could lead to a danger of developing osteoporosis (loss of bone density) in later years.

Make sure you consume enough foods that are rich in calcium, such as dairy products or salmon. You may want to take calcium supplements, even in a simple form such as an antacid, to make sure your intake is adequate. Again, make sure to consult your physician before taking this step.

Performance-Enhancing Substances

Once the domain of professional and elite athletes, substances such as steroids and other legal and illegal performance enhancers have trickled down to the college and high school level over the years. Most of these are banned by various professional leagues and athletic governing bodies, and cautionary tales about their often dangerous side effects abound. Yet this has not stopped many younger athletes from experimenting with them.

Following are descriptions of some common performance-enhancing substances and their side effects.

STEROIDS

Anabolic steroids, which are the synthetic derivatives of male hormones, have been shown to increase lean muscle mass, and therefore are often used by athletes in sports that require strength, such as football. They also are illegal, banned by virtually every professional and amateur athletic organization because of their dangerous side effects, which include liver damage, elevated blood pressure, mood swings and aggression, heart disease, and impaired immune function.

Since anabolic steroids increase the levels of testosterone in the blood, they can have the effect of causing masculine characteristics in women, such as increased muscularity, deepening of the voice, and increased facial hair.

HUMAN GROWTH HORMONE (HGH)

Human growth hormone is a hormone produced in the body by the pituitary gland that is thought to enhance performance when taken in higher concentrations, usually by injection. It is banned by the major international sports governing bodies, but it is believed to be widely used in some sports and is very difficult to detect accurately. Increasing the level of HGH in your body is thought to increase your protein retention, which may give you a slight advantage in terms of adding muscle. But the advantage is minor compared to the potential side effects of taking too much HGH: excessive perspiration, hypertension or high blood pressure, diabetes, widening of the jaw, enlarged facial features, and arthritis.

CREATINE AND ANDROSTENEDIONE

Creatine, or creatine monohydrate, is an over-the-counter supplement in powder form that assists in the production of ADP (adenosine diphosphate) in the muscles and enables the muscles to work harder. It has been shown to help athletes gain more muscle, power, and mass, and is reportedly used by many professional athletes. However, many professional teams have banned its use because of reports of side effects such as headaches, stomach cramps, elevated blood pressure, and severe muscle cramps.

Androstenedione, or "andro," a supplement taken in pill form, received a great deal of publicity in 1998 when it was discovered that baseball slugger Mark McGwire was taking the substance during his quest for the all-time single-season home run record. Although classified as a dietary supplement, andro actually simulates anabolic steroids and has been shown in studies to increase the level of testosterone in the blood and thus aid in increasing muscular development. However, a 1999 study published in the *Journal of the American Medical Association* found not only that it did not increase testosterone levels, but that it actually increased the levels of estrogen, or female hormones, in the male subjects. It also raised cholesterol levels in the blood.

Fortunately, along with the explosion of supplements and performance-enhancing substances on the market has come a corresponding wealth of literature detailing the potential dangers inherent in their use. Any athlete, no matter what level of experience or ability, should make herself fully aware of the risks before even considering using any supplement.

13

EXERCISES—
DESCRIPTIONS
AND TECHNIQUES

This chapter describes the exercises listed in the Preparatory and Sport-Specific programs in Chapters 7, 9, 10, 11, 12, and 13. These pictures and descriptions are meant to be used as a guide. You should always consult with your coach or trainer before attempting a new exercise, and you should perform exercises with a spotter where noted and under the supervision of qualified personnel. Take full advantage of safety features such as weight belts or seatbelts on weight machines whenever you are doing any exercise that puts stress on your lower back.

Step-up with acceleration

Accelerated step-up: Hold the bar on your shoulders (or hold light dumbbells in your hands, behind your head). Lean forward and step up on the box with one leg explosively, then bring your other leg up onto the box and raise your knee as high as you can before bringing it back

Alternate leg/arm twisting crunch

Back extension

down. Step back down slowly, under control with a soft landing. Caution: do not attempt this exercise without a spotter, even if you have mastered the technique.

Alternate leg/arm twisting crunch: Lie on the floor with your hands crossed in front of your chest and your knees bent. Raise yourself up and twist so that you can touch your left knee with your right elbow. Alternate with your left elbow to your right knee.

Back extension: Hold your hands across your chest (some people like to hold a weight) with your feet flat on the floor or pad. Bend forward as far as is comfortable and then back up to the starting position, making sure not to arch your back.

Back squat: Hold the bar with your palms pointed forward, your elbows flexed and up and the bar resting on your shoulders behind your head. Keep your elbows raised and your upper arms as close to parallel with the floor as possible, and your feet shoulder-width apart (or slightly wider). Slowly lower the bar by bending at the knees while keeping

**Balance ball, push-up,
feet on ball**

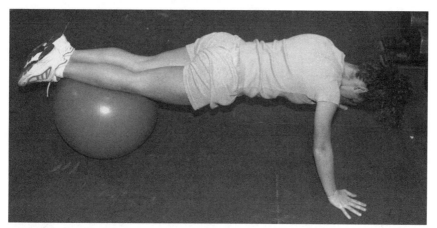

Balance ball, push-up, legs on ball

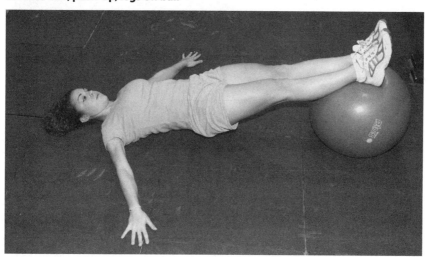

Balance ball, hamstrings

your back straight. Your weight should be over the middle of your feet and back, not over your toes, and your heels should stay flat on the ground. Lower yourself until the tops of your thighs are parallel to the floor. Keeping your head pointed forward, slowly raise back up by straightening your legs, making sure not to point your knees outward.

Balance ball abs: Assume a push-up position with your legs on the balance ball. Bring your knees up toward your waist, then extend your legs back.

Balance ball hamstrings: Lie on your back with your legs on top of the balance ball. Roll the ball toward your body, keeping your calves and heels on the ball as you bring your knees up. To help your balance, keep your arms flat on the ground at a 45-degree angle to your body.

Balance ball incline press with dumbbell: Lie on the ball so that the middle of your back is supported and your feet are apart. With a dumbbell in each hand and your elbows bent about 90 degrees, bring your hands together until they almost meet, then move them back to the starting position.

Balance ball push-up: Assume a push-up position with your hands on the balance ball. Widen your hands if you have

Balance ball, hamstrings

Incline press with dumbbell (center and bottom photos)

Balance ball, push-up, hands on ball

Bench press (above and following pages)

trouble balancing. Do a regular push-up, keeping your legs extended. For a modified version, extend your legs on the balance ball and do a regular push-up.

Bench press: Keep your back flat on the bench with your feet flat on the floor and a normal arch in your lower back. Do not arch your back or neck while you are lifting, as this can lead to injury. Rest the bar lightly on your chest and grasp it with your palms turned upward and your hands a little wider than shoulder-width apart. Use a fluid motion to lift the bar up and slightly back, so when you are extending your arms the bar is above your eyes. Lower it slowly back to your chest.

90-degree bench press: Keep your upper back and head flat on the bench and your feet flat on the floor. Do not arch your back or neck while you are lifting, as this can lead to injury. Grasp the bar with your palms turned upward and your hands a little wider than shoulder-width apart. Use a fluid motion to lift the bar up and slightly back, so when you are extending your arms the bar is above your shoulders. Lower the bar until your elbows are bent at a 90-degree angle, but not lower. Some athletes put a rolled-up towel on their chest and make sure the bar doesn't touch the towel.

Bent-over row: Stand with your feet shoulder-width apart and hold the bar with your palms facing down and your elbows and knees bent slightly. Bend over in hang position while keeping your upper back straight and lock in your lower back (natural arch) and let the bar hang down. Raise the bar back up to your chest in this position, then lower it back down. Use of a lifting belt is highly recommended, especially while you are learning the exercise.

Biceps curl: Stand upright with your feet shoulder-width apart, and your hands holding the bar slightly wider than your feet and with your palms facing upward. The bar should rest on the front of your thighs and your upper arms should be against your ribs. Flex your arms at the elbows and raise the bar until it is a few inches from your chest. Keep your el-

Bench Press (this page and opposite)

Bench press

bows and upper arms stationary during the entire motion. Slowly lower the bar back down to the starting position.

Butt kicks: Run in place, swinging your arms in a controlled motion. Kick your legs back up behind you so that your heels lightly touch your buttocks.

Crunches: Lie on your back on the floor with your legs bent and feet on the floor, or with your legs on a bench or chair. Fold your arms across your chest. Keeping your lower back stationary, curl your trunk upward and raise your head and shoulders off the ground. Slowly return to the starting position.

Bent over row

Biceps curls

Dead lift with hex bar: Stand with your feet about shoulder-width apart. Grip the sides of the hex bar and squat down, keeping your back straight, shoulders back, lower back locked, and your head forward. Slowly straighten your legs and hips as you pull the bar up past your knees until you are back to a standing position, then return the weight to the floor while bending your knees slowly and keeping your back straight. (Hint: This exercise can be simulated on Universal weight machine using the bench press. Remove the bench and stand on top of a box facing the bar that is high enough so that you have to squat down to reach the bar. Repeat the exercise as described above.) Use of a lifting belt is highly recommended, especially while you are learning the exercise.

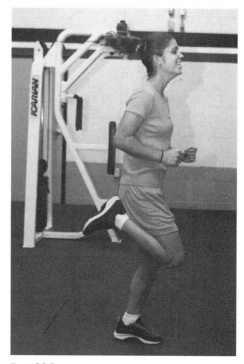

Butt kick

Dead lift with hex bar (above and right)

Bench dips

Dip

Dot drill

Dips (regular): Lift yourself above the bars with your arms straight, then slowly lower yourself down until your armpits are almost touching the bars. Lift yourself back up by extending your arms. You can cross your feet together to keep your legs from splaying apart.

Form running drill, arm swing

45-degree lunge

Dips (modified): Place two benches parallel to each other, about three or four feet apart. With your feet on one bench and your hands on the other, lower and raise yourself with your arms.

Dot drill: There are six basic variations for this drill that use one leg or both legs. Ask your coach or trainer for these variations. (Both feet, one foot, hopscotch, etc.)

Form running (arm swings): Stand with your feet flat and shoulder-width apart, and hold a one- or two-pound weight in each hand. Swing your arms back and forth as if you are running. Concentrate on good form and keeping in control.

45-degree lunge: Use the same technique as the front lunge, but step forward with your front leg at a 45-degree angle to your body.

Front lunge: Hold the bar behind your head so it rests on your shoulders, or hold the dumbbells at your side. Keep your back straight and step forward with one leg, and bend your front knee, but do not extend your front knee beyond your toe. Your back knee should almost touch the ground. Raise back up to the starting position by pushing off from your leg. Alternate legs for each repetition.

Front squat: Hold the bar with your palms pointed forward and your elbows flexed and up so that the bar rest on the front of your shoulders,

Front lunge

under your chin. Keep your elbows raised and your upper arms as close to parallel with the floor as possible, and your feet shoulder-width apart (or slightly wider). Slowly lower the bar by bending at the knees while keeping your back straight. Your weight should be over the middle of your feet and back, not over your toes, and your heels should stay flat on the ground. Lower yourself until the tops of your thighs are parallel to the floor. Keeping your head pointed forward, slowly raise back up by straightening your legs and extending your hips, making sure not to point your knees outward. Use of a lifting belt is highly recommended, especially while you are learning the exercise.

Good morning: While standing upright, hold the barbell on your shoulders, behind your head. In one fluid motion, bend forward at the waist

Front squat (above and right)

while keeping your head upright, then return back to an upright position. Since this exercise can potentially place great stress on your lower back, use a low weight and proceed gradually when adding weight. Use of a lifting belt is highly recommended, especially while you are learning the exercise.

Hang clean: Use a motion similar to a dead lift with the hex bar. With your feet shoulder-width apart and the bar on the floor just over your second shoelace, squat down with your back straight and grasp the bar with your palms pointed downward. Your hands should be slightly

Good morning (below and right)

Hang clean (above, opposite, and following page)

Hang clean

wider than shoulder width, and your elbows should point out slightly to the sides. Lean forward so your shoulders are over the bar, keeping your back straight. In a fluid motion, straighten up by extending your knees, moving your hips forward and lifting the bar with your arms extended. When in the hang position, rest the bar on the front of your thighs near or above your kneecap. Leaning forward slightly, but still with your back straight, shoulders back and a natural arch in your lower back, extend your hips, knees, and ankle upward, as if you are jumping with the weight. Keep your arms extended with your elbows

Hang clean

out to the side and the bar close to your body for the first part of the motion, then pull the bar upward toward your chest as you rotate your elbows under the bar. You should end up catching with the bar resting on the front of your shoulders with your palms facing upward, elbows pointing forward, and your wrists extended. Slowly, lower the bar back down so that it is resting on your thighs, keeping your back straight. Never attempt this exercise without supervision. Use of a lifting belt is highly recommended, especially while you are learning the exercise.

High knees: Run in place, swinging your arms in a controlled manner as you are running. Lift your knees high off the ground as you are run-

Form running drill, high knees

ning, making sure to land on your toes or on the balls of your feet. Concentrate on your balance, and get into a rhythm by doing a small bounce or hop on each step.

High pull: Stand in the hang ready position holding the bar on your thighs, near the knees, with your palms facing back and knuckles down, as you would to perform a power shrug. As you begin to pull the bar upward toward your shoulders, extend your knees while thrusting your hips forward, and rise on your toes. At completion of the pull to your shoulders, lower the bar back to the starting position while lowering your heels back onto the floor.

Hip abduction/adduction: Sit with your back flush against the seat. Use the seatbelt to keep your lower back from arching. For hip abduction, start with your legs together and push outward, pause, and slowly bring back together. For hip adduction, start with your legs apart and bring together, pause, then push apart. Try not to tense your muscles.

Hip-leg abduction (above and top of following page)

Incline (bench) press (above and right)

Incline press: The bench should be tilted at about a 45-degree angle to the floor. Keep your back flat on the bench with your feet flat on the floor and a natural arch in your lower back. Do not arch your back or neck while you are lifting, as this can lead to injury. Rest the bar

Hip-leg adduction (above and below)

lightly on your chest and grasp it with your palms turned upward and your hands a little wider than shoulder-width apart. Use a fluid motion to lift the bar up and slightly back, so when you are extending your arms straight up the bar is above your eyes. Lower it slowly back to your chest. Use a spotter for this exercise.

Lat pulls (wide grip): Hold the bar with your palms facing forward and your arms fully extended. Lean back slightly as you pull down on the bar until it touches your breastbone. Slowly let the bar back up to the

Lat pull down to chest, wide grip (above and right)

Lat pull down to chest, close grip

start position. Avoid arching your back.

Lat pulls (close grip): Hold the bar with your palms facing back toward you. Pull the bar down as you drive your elbows down and back. Slowly let the bar back up to the start position.

Leg curls: Lie face-down on the bench with your kneecaps off the back end and your lower legs touching the pads. With your hands holding the bars on either side, lift the weight by flexing your knees until just before the pads touch your buttocks. Slowly lower the weight back to the starting position. Do not arch your back.

Leg extension: Keep your back flush against the seat. Use a seatbelt if one is available. Your knees should be off the edge of the seat. Lift the weight by extending your knees (they should be fully extended at the

Leg curl (above and center)

Leg extension

top of the motion). Slowly bring back to the starting position.

Low row: From a sitting position with your arms extended, pull the weight back to your chest as you flex your elbows. Try not to lean forward too much. Keep your back straight with a natural arch in your lower back. Do not arch your back. Return the weight to the starting position.

Lunge jumps: Start with your arms at your sides. Jump and scissor your legs so you land with them apart, one in front of the other. Repeat, and focus on balance by keeping your arms in a running position.

Medicine ball foot toss (seated): Sit on the floor with your knees bent and

Low row

Lunge jumps (above and bottom two figures)

the medicine ball between your feet. Toss the ball high enough so your partner can catch it without bending over. You may want to try balancing the ball on the tops of your feet.

Medicine ball, seated foot toss (above and below)

Medicine ball lunge with twist to front leg: Hold a medicine ball close to your body at chest level. Do a front lunge as described, and twist your upper body to one side while holding the ball. Repeat and twist to the other side.

Medicine ball seated crunch twist: Sit on the floor in a sit-up position with your knees bent and your feet on the floor. Holding the medicine ball with both hands, twist to either side and touch the ball to the ground. As you improve, do the exercise with your feet slightly off the floor.

Medicine ball, lunge with twist to front leg

Medicine ball seated side throw: Sit on the floor with your knees bent. Hold the ball with both hands on the floor on your right side (if you are right-handed). Rotate your trunk and throw the ball with a sideward motion to a partner or against the wall. As you improve, move farther away from the target.

Medicine ball standing side throw: Stand in a ready stance holding the ball in both hands on your right side (if you are right-handed). Pivot with your back foot, throwing the ball with both hands as if you are swinging a bat. Stand at least 10 feet away from your target.

Medicine ball sumo swing to eye height: Squat down holding the ball with both hands between your knees. As you straighten your knees and rise up, hold the ball out in front of you with both hands until it reaches eye level.

Medicine ball trunk twist: Hold the ball with both hands with your arms slightly bent. Twist to either side, moving your head so you are always keeping your eyes on the ball.

One-leg squat to cone touch: Stand on one leg, squat down with your nonstanding leg bent and extended behind you, and lean forward and touch the top of the cone with your hand. Raise back up until you are standing upright on one leg.

One-leg squat to toe raise: Hold a small medicine ball at chest level with both hands. Standing on one leg, squat down, then straighten up as you raise the ball above your

Medicine ball, seated crunch twist

Medicine ball, seated side throw (above and right)

Medicine ball, standing throw (above and right)

head. You should end up on your toes with your arms fully extended over your head.

Pec fly: Sit with your back flush against the seat and your hands at about chest level. Starting with your arms apart, bring your arms

Medicine ball sumo swing to eye height

One-leg squat to cone touch

together until they almost touch. Slowly return to the start position. Your elbows should be facing out with a slight bend back and not quite locked.

Plyometric sit-up: Lie on your back with your partner standing behind your head. Keeping your abdominal muscles tight, lift your legs up to where your partner can push them back down, either to one side or straight. Stop your legs about six inches before they touch the ground.

One-leg squat to layups (above and right)

Pec fly (above and following page)

Power shrug/high pull: Stand in ready position holding the bar on your thighs near or above your knees with your palms facing back. Thrust hips forward as you extend your knees and shrug your shoulders while

Pec fly

Plyometric sit-up

Power shrug/high pull (above, right, and following page)

raising up on your toes, keeping your arms extended. Concentrate on lifting the bar with your shoulders, not with your arms. Use of a lifting bar is highly recommended, especially while you are learning the exercise.

Preacher curls: Lean forward slightly with your back straight and your arms flush against the pad. Flex your elbows and bring the weight up slowly, then back down to the starting position.

Pullover: Lie on a bench and hold the bar behind your head. With your elbows bent, bring the bar over your head to above your chest, then back to the starting position. Use a spotter for this exercise.

Pull-ups (modified, with box): Stand on the box and let yourself hang from the bar with your palms facing forward. Lift yourself up so your chin is over the bar. The spotter can hold your lower back or waist if necessary. Try not to let your legs swing back and forth.

Push press: Bring the bar up to your shoulders with the technique used in hang clean exercise. With the bar resting on your shoulders and your elbows in toward your body,

Power shrug/high pull

Preacher curls (above and right)

Bench press, closed grip (above and below)

rotate your shoulders to point forward. Flex your hips and knees slightly. Push the bar upward in an explosive, controlled movement until your elbows are fully extended. As you do this, extend your knees and move your body weight to the balls of your feet, and raise your heels off the ground slightly. When the bar is fully extended above you, make sure your feet are back flat on the ground. Lower the bar slowly to your shoulders, flexing your hips and knees slightly as the bar touches your shoulders. Use of a lifting belt is highly recommended, especially while you are learning the exercise.

Push-up: Start with your legs extended and arms perpendicular to the floor, with your body at a 30-degree angle to the floor. Flex your arms,

Pull-up

keeping your elbows close to your sides, and lower your body until your upper arm is parallel to the floor and your body is two inches off the floor. Extend your arms to push your body back up to the starting position.

Push-up to T stance: Perform a regular push-up, but as you extend your arms and rise up, rotate your body and raise one arm upward, balancing yourself on the other arm so your arms are in a T position. Bring your arm back down to the floor and repeat.

Push-up with clap: Perform a push-up as described above, but as you push your body back up to the starting position, raise your hands off the

Push press (above and right)

Push-up (above and center)

Push-up to T stance

Rear delt (top two photos)

Romanian dead lift (above and right)

floor and clap them together and end in the bottom push-up position. Make sure to do the clap as you are near the starting position so you have time to clap and get your hands back on the floor.

Rear delt: Sit with your back flush against the seat and your hands at about chest level. Starting with your hands together, move them apart with your arms slightly bent. Do not let your arms go beyond a position parallel to your shoulders.

Romanian dead lift: Stand upright with your feet flat and shoulder- or hip-width apart. Hold the bar with your palms facing back and knuckles pointing down. Bend your knees slightly, inhale, and hold your breath as you lower the bar close to the middle of your shin by bending from the hip. Exhale as you complete the movement. As you descend, your hips should go back to maintain your center of gravity as you bend forward. Keep your head forward with your shoulders back (spread chest). Your lower back should be tight and locked with a normal curve (slight arch). Raise the bar back up by keeping your spine in position, pulling your torso up and pushing your hips forward.

Rotator cuff exercise (internal rotation): Lie on your back holding a dumbbell in your throwing hand. Keep your arm bent at a 90-degree angle and close to your side. Starting with your arm pointed straight up, slowly lower the dumbbell to your side, then return it to the starting position.

Rotator cuff exercise (external rotation): Lie on your side with your head resting on one arm. With your other arm at a 90-degree angle and your elbow close to your body, start with the dumbbell pointing away

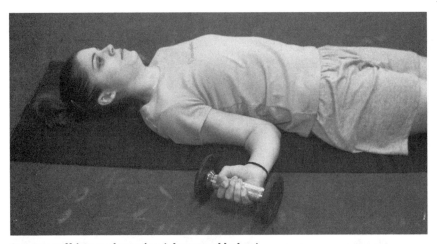

Rotator cuff, internal rotation (above and below)

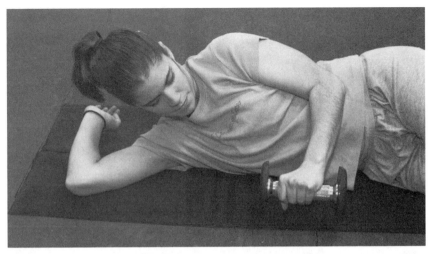

Rotator cuff, external rotation (this page and following page)

from your body and slowly bring it back toward your chest. Raise back to the starting position.

Rotator cuff exercise: Lie on your back with your throwing arm on the floor and bent at a 90-degree angle. Slowly lift the dumbbell to a vertical position, then past vertical as long as it feels comfortable. Return to the starting position.

Seated calf: Sit with your back straight (but not arched) and with your toes on the pads. The weights should be snug against your thighs. Push

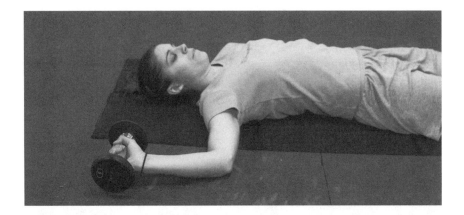

with your toes so your heels raise off the pads, then slowly lower back down.

Seated leg curl: Sit with your back flush against the pad and your calves against the leg pads. Use a seatbelt if one is available to keep your back from arching. Start with your legs extended and flex them while holding on to the side bars. Slowly bring your legs back up to the starting position.

Shoulder press: This exercise should be performed with a spotter. Sit on the bench and hold the bar so that it is resting on the front of your shoulders, under your chin. Grip it with your palms facing forward and your wrists slightly extended. Keeping your back as straight as possible and bending your knees slightly, slowly push the bar upward until your arms are extended. While you are doing this, keep your elbows pointed out to the side until you reach full extension. Do not lock your elbows. Slowly lower the bar back down to the starting position.

Seated leg curl (above and right)

Shoulder press (above and right)

Shoulder raise with dumbbell: Stand in the ready position and hold the dumbbells with your palms facing toward your body. With your arms slightly bent, slowly raise the dumbbells until they are at shoulder height, then lower them back to your sides.

Shrug: Use the same technique as the power shrug, but keep your feet flat on the ground instead of raising up on your toes. You should be in a high play position, which means your knees should have about a 10-degree bend, your lower back should have its natural arch, and your shoulders should be back. Your body weight should be on the middle or the balls of your feet. This posture is used for shrugs and standing rows. Depending on your arm length, the bar should rest on your upper thigh.

Shoulder raises with dumbbell

Side lunge: Start in the same position as the front lunge and 45-degree lunge, but step to the side, bending your front leg and extending your back leg behind you. You can let your back foot roll over to get more extension. Alternate legs for each repetition.

Single row with dumbbell: Stand with one knee on a bench and one on the ground. Hold a dumbbell in one hand and lean over, making sure to keep your back straight and your shoulders square. Start with your arm extended and lift the dumbbell up as high as you can while bending your elbow, then lower it back down.

Sit-up: Lie on your back with your knees bent and your feet flat on the floor. Fold your arms across your chest. Raise your head and shoulders

Side lunge

Single row with dumbbell (above and right)

until your arms touch your thighs. Slowly return to the starting position.

Snatch high pull: This is one of the most difficult lifts, and should not be attempted without supervision and spotters. Stand with your feet flat and about shoulder width apart, and your toes pointing slightly outward. The bar should be over the balls of your feet. Lock in your lower back and spread your chest, bend at the knees and grasp the bar with your palms facing down. The hand grip is wider than the regular high pull, with the grip near the end of the bar. Keeping your arms straight, lift the bar to just above your knees by extending your knees and shift your weight to the rear part of your foot. Move your hips forward so your thighs make light contact with the bar near your knees. In the hang position, as you continue to lift the bar upward past your waist, extend your body fully—knees, hips, and thighs—as if you are jumping off the ground. Shrug your shoulders and pull you body under the bar. Keep your elbows pointing out and your wrists in position until the bar is near your shoulders. Keep your elbows high. Slowly return to hang position. Use of a lifting belt is highly recommended, especially while you are learning the exercise.

Squat: Start in an upright position with your feet a little wider than shoulder-width apart in the ready position with your toes pointed out-

Snatch high pull

ward slightly. Rest the bar on your shoulders behind your head, with your palms facing forward. Inhale as you slowly squat down until your thighs are just about parallel to the floor, keeping your head facing forward and your lower back straight or with natural arch. Your weight should be distributed on the middle of your feet with heels on the ground. Also, your knees should track in the same direction as your feet and should not extend forward beyond your feet. Raise your body back up to the starting position and exhale as you go beyond the sticking point. Hint: Unlike the bench press or other exercises, the second, upward part of the motion should be faster than the first.

Squat (above and following page)

Squat

Squat jump: Start with your hands on your hips. Bend your knees, jump, and land, bending your knees as you land. Repeat, and focus on being on the ground for as short a time as possible between jumps.

Squat thrust: Stand with your feet together and hands at your sides. In one continuous motion, squat down, steadying yourself with your hands, then extend your legs behind so you are in a push-up position. Bring your legs back up underneath you as they were, then stand upright.

Squat with wooden dowel: You can use the wooden dowel to practice your technique for the different lifts such as squats, hang cleans, and dead lifts.

Squat jump (above and right)

Standing calf: Perform this exercise with a squat rack and with spotters, if necessary. You will also need a slightly raised surface, such as a flat board, to be placed in front of your feet. Grip the bar with your palms pointing forward and hold it behind your head, at the base of your neck. Place the balls of your feet on the edge of the board or raised surface. Keep your feet pointing straight ahead and straighten your knees until they are bent slightly. Slowly push up on your toes and hold this position for a few seconds, then lower your heels back down so they are below the level of your toes.

Standing row: Stand with your feet shoulder-width apart and your head facing forward. Hold the bar with your palms facing back. Lift the bar to your chest, keeping your elbows high. Hold for a second and slowly lower back down to the starting position.

Step-up: Hold the bar behind your head in a back squat position. Lean forward and step up on the box with one leg, then bring your other leg up onto the box. Step back down while leaning on the lead leg, then slowly lower other leg to the ground with minimum impact. Caution: Do not attempt this exercise without a spotter, even if you have mastered the technique.

Squat thrust (left and below)

Squat with wooden dowel

Standing calf (above and below)

Standing row

Triceps (close grip bench press): Lie on a bench and hold the bar with your elbows bent and your hands close together. Start with the bar on your chest and raise it directly above your shoulders. Lower it slowly back to the starting position. Use a spotter for this exercise.

Step-up (above and right)

Triceps (extension): Lie on a bench and hold the bar with your arms tight to your sides and your hands and elbows close together. Start with the bar behind your head and bring it up over your head, then return it to the starting position. Use a spotter for this exercise.

Triceps (French curl): Hold a single dumbbell with both hands. Start with your hands just above your head and slowly bring them behind your head before returning the weight back to the starting position. Keep elbows pointing forward. Use a spotter for this exercise.

Twisting sit-ups: Lie on your back with your knees bent and your arms folded across your chest. Raise your torso up and twist to the left so your right elbow touches your left knee. Lower yourself back down, then repeat, twisting to the right this time.

Upper back pull-up from squat rack: With your feet on the floor and your arms and legs extended, grab the bar and pull yourself up as if you are doing a pull-up. Slowly lower yourself back down.

Wall push-up: Stand far enough away from a wall so you have to lean forward a little with your arms extended to touch your palms against the wall. Lean forward and do a push-up against the wall by flexing your arms and then pushing your body back by extending your arms.

Wrist curl: Sit with your arms resting on your thighs and your hands extended past your knees. Using a barbell or dumbbells, lower the

Bench press, close grip

Triceps extension with barbell, closed grip (above and below)

Tricep extension (French curl) with dumbbell (above and right)

Upper-back pull-ups from squat rack

Twisting sit-up

Wrist curls (above and below)

weight as far as you can just by bending your wrists, then raise it back to the starting position. Do this using both the regular (palms up) and reverse (palms down) grip. Another way to strengthen your wrists and forearms is by doing lateral wrist curls, in which you use a dumbbell that has a weight attached to one end. Holding the dumbbell in the middle with the weight facing up, rotate the bar to the side and then back to the upright position.

GLOSSARY

abdominal muscles   The muscles that lie between your thorax and pelvis: the rectus abdominis and the external obliques.

abduction   To draw away from the midpoint of the body. When performing hip abduction exercises, you start with your legs together and move one or both outward.

acetylcholine   A chemical that is released when nerve impulses are sent to your muscles and causes the muscle to contract.

active rest   A training phase in which you do not perform resistance exercises, but instead pursue other sports activities that may be unrelated to your specific sport.

adduction   To draw inward toward the middle of the body. When performing hip adduction exercises, you start with your legs apart and move one or both inward.

adenosine triphosphate (ATP)   An energy-storing molecule that provides the energy used in muscle contraction. Muscular activity requires a constant supply of ATP.

aerobic exercises/training   Training that is designed to improve your body's circulatory and respiratory efficiency through sustained, vigorous exercise.

amino acids   Organic compounds that, when linked together by peptide bonds, form proteins.

anaerobic exercises/training   Training that focuses on short, explosive actions. Sprinting is a classic example of an anaerobic activity.

androstenedione   A performance-enhancing supplement that has been shown to have similar effects to anabolic steroids, that is, it increases the level of testosterone in the blood.

anemia   A low red blood cell count, reflecting a deficiency in the oxygen-carrying component of the blood. Anemia can be avoided by eating an iron-rich diet.

antibodies   Protein substances produced in your body that weaken or neutralize bacteria or toxins.

barbell   A bar with adjustable weights at each end used in weight lifting.

biaxial joint   A joint that allows two types of movement. Your wrist and ankle are biaxial joints.

biceps   The muscle at the front of your upper arm that flexes your forearm.

blood-sugar level   The concentration of glucose in the blood, measured in milligrams of glucose per 100 milliliters of blood.

calcium   A mineral found in dairy and other foods that contributes to healthy bones and teeth. Lack of calcium can lead to osteoporosis (decreased bone density).

calorie   A unit of energy-producing potential that is contained in food and released upon oxidation by the body.

carbohydrates (simple and complex)   Group of organic compounds that, when broken down by the body, become glucose molecules which the body can use for energy. Simple carbohydrates include refined sugars and sugars that occur naturally. Complex carbohydrates are found in breads, pasta, fruits, and vegetables.

cardiovascular exercise   Any exercise that raises your heart rate and gets blood flowing to your muscles and joints.

concentric action   The shortening of the muscles that occurs when you are lifting a weight.

cool-down   A post-workout routine that lets your body make the transition from being stressed to being at rest. This helps your muscles remove some of the lactic acid buildup after a strenuous workout.

creatine   An over-the-counter supplement that assists in the production of ADP (adenosine diphosphate) in the muscles and enables the muscles to work harder. Creatine has been banned by many pro sports teams.

cross training   Training that combines different types of aerobic, anaerobic, and resistance exercises.

dead-lift grip   Holding a barbell with one palm facing up and the other palm facing down.

detraining   The decrease in strength and conditioning that occurs when you suspend your training program.

dietary/nutritional supplements   Minerals, amino acids, or other substances that do not claim to have any specific therapeutic value and thus are not regulated by the Food and Drug Administration (FDA).

dumbbell   A short weight bar that is used in exercises such as wrist curls or biceps curls. Usually comes in different weights, but may include adjustable weights.

dynamic muscle action   A resistance exercise that involves motion, such as raising a weight (concentric action) and bringing it back down (eccentric action).

eccentric action   The lengthening of the muscles that occurs during deceleration, such as bringing a weight back down to its starting position.

elasticity system   A system of springs or rubber bands used in many home gym units. These exercises provide low resistance at the beginning of the motion and high resistance toward the end.

endurance training   See AEROBIC TRAINING.

estrogen   Hormones produced mainly by the ovaries that are responsible for the development and maintenance of female secondary sex characteristics.

explosive exercises   Exercises that focus on short, explosive movements such as jumping, lunging, and sprinting, and that use maximal or near-maximal force.

extension   Moving your limb or joint from a bent to a straight position.

fast-twitch muscle fibers   Muscle fibers that develop force quickly over a short period of time. They allow you to sprint and accelerate.

FDA   U.S. Food and Drug Administration, the government agency that sets and enforces standards for the production and sale of food and drugs.

flexion   Moving your limb or joint from a straight to a bent position.

fluid resistance   The type of resistance employed in exercise machines that use cylinders and pistons rather than traditional weights.

free weights   Dumbbells, barbells, and plates that are not attached to pulleys, pistons, or other apparatus. They allow a greater range of motion than weight machines, but require more focus on technique and balance.

friction resistance   The type of resistance employed in some exercise machines, such as some cycling machines.

glucose   A blood sugar that is the major source of energy in the body.

glycemic index   A system that measures how quickly a food is converted to glucose in the bloodstream.

hamstring   The three muscles (semitendinosus, semimembranosus, and biceps femoris) that run along the back of your thigh and that you use to flex your knee and extend your thigh.

high play position   Knees have about a 10-degree bend, the lower back has its natural arch, and shoulders are back. Body weight is on the middle or the balls of the feet. This posture is the one used for shrugs and standing rows. Depending on arm length, the bar will rest on upper thigh.

hormones   Substances produced in the body that affect physiological activity such as growth or metabolism.

human growth hormone (HGH)   A hormone produced in the body by the pituitary gland that is thought to enhance performance when taken in higher concentrations, usually by injection. It is banned by the major international sports governing bodies.

hypertrophy   An increase in muscle size.

in-season   An extended period that features regular competition.

intensity   The percentage of your repetition maximum (RM) that you use during a workout.

isolation (of muscles)   Focusing on a specific muscle or muscle group and performing exercises to overload it.

isometric muscle action   Any exercise in which you are pushing against an immovable object.

lactic acid   Liquid produced by intense anaerobic activity that can build up in your muscles and cause fatigue.

latissimus dorsi (lats)   The muscles just below your shoulder blades that extend to your sides.

ligaments   Tissues that connect bones to other bones.

macrocycle   One full year of your training program, usually beginning and ending with the conclusion of a season.

medicine ball   A large, heavy ball, usually bound in leather, that is used in conditioning exercises.

mesocycle   In periodized weight training, the different phases of a macrocycle: Functional Strength Base, Preparatory, Hypertrophy, and Strength and Power.

microcycle   A one- to two-week phase of a mesocycle.

minerals   Essential nutritional elements, such as calcium, iron, potassium, or sodium.

motor nerves/neurons   Neurons that convey impulses from your central nervous system to your muscles.

motor unit   The combination of a motor nerve and the muscle fibers to which it is attached.

multiaxial joint   A body joint that allows movement in three directions. Your shoulder, hip, and knee are multiaxial joints.

multiple-joint exercises   Exercises that put stress on more than one joint. Examples of these are back squats and dead lifts.

muscle fibers   The cells that make up your muscles. They are long, cylindrical cells about the diameter of a human hair, and are grouped in bundles of up to 150 called fasciculi.

muscle group   A group of muscles that combines to perform a particular function. For example, your quadriceps, or thigh muscles, are a muscle group made up of four muscles—the rectus femoris, vastus lateralis, vastus medialis, and vastus intermedialis—that enable you to flex your hips and extend your knees.

muscle imbalance   The result of strengthening some muscle groups at the expense of others, such as by doing one type of activity or sport to the exclusion of others.

muscular endurance   The ability of a muscle or muscle group to contract repeatedly for an extended period, such as during sit-ups.

nonresistance training Exercises that do not involve the use of weights, such as sit-ups, push-ups, and jumping jacks.

nutrients Sources of nourishment found in food.

off-season Extended period when no competition takes place.

osteoporosis Loss of bone density. More common in women than in men, and in older women, though it can affect younger women as well.

overload The act of forcing your muscles to do more than they used to doing, which enables you to increase your muscle size and strength.

overtraining A condition unique to athletes in which excessive training causes fatigue, mood swings, depression, and altered sleeping and eating habits.

performance-enhancing supplement Any substance that is used specifically to improve or enhance performance.

periodization A system of training that varies the intensity of your workouts and alternates the exercises you perform over a period of weeks and months.

phosphagen Energy-supplying chemical composed of creatine and phosphate produced during the breakdown of adenosine triphosphate (ATP) during anaerobic activity. Phosphagens are thought to support high-intensity anaerobic activity for approximately six to 10 seconds.

plyometrics Exercises using high-speed movements that allow a muscle to achieve maximal strength in as short a time as possible.

power The rate of force (force times speed), or how fast you are able to move an object.

power position A power position like the hang position is used when performing power shrugs and high pulls. Your knees should have about a 30-degree bend so that, depending on arm length, the bar will rest from just below your knee to mid-thigh. Your lower back should have its natural arch and your shoulders should be back. Your body weight should be on the middle to the balls of your feet.

preparatory phase A mesocycle of a periodized weight training program that prepares your muscles and joints for overloading in the next phase of doing multiple-joint resistance exercises with minimal overload.

proteins Fundamental components of all living cells that supply amino acids, assist in the formation of hormones and enzymes, and aid the development of antibodies.

quadriceps The four muscles in the front of your thigh that attach to the quadriceps tendon, which attaches to your kneecap. When you flex your quadriceps muscles, the quadriceps tendon is what allows them to pull on the kneecap and straighten your leg.

range of motion   The normal movements your joints make. Regaining range of motion is one of the first steps in rehabilitating an injury.

recovery   The period between exercises or between workouts during which your body adapts to the stresses imposed by resistance training.

repetition maximum (RM)   The maximum number of repetitions you can perform at a certain weight. For example, if you can bench press 100 pounds 10 times but no more, your 10RM for the bench press is 100.

repetitions   The number of times you lift a weight during one set. Also referred to as reps.

resistance training   Training that requires the exertion of force against a movable or immovable object.

rest period   The time you take between sets, usually ranging from 30 seconds to three or four minutes.

rotator cuff   Four muscles that originate at the shoulder blade and form one continuous cuff that controls the rotation of the ball-shaped head of the upper arm bone in the shoulder socket and keeps the ball centered in the socket as it is rotating.

set   A group of repetitions of a specific exercise that is followed by a short rest period.

single-joint exercises   Exercises that allow movement at only one joint and usually train only one muscle group; for example, arm curls and knee extensions.

slow-twitch muscle fibers   Muscle fibers that develop force slowly and over a long period of time. They give you energy and endurance during aerobic activities.

specificity   Tailoring your training program to the specific sport(s) you play by adding, subtracting, or altering exercises.

sports drinks   Specially manufactured drinks that contain extra carbohydrates.

spotter   A person who assists the lifter during an exercise, particularly if the exercise involves heavy weights or is technically difficult.

squat rack   A rack on either side of the lifter that holds the barbell. This makes it easier for the lifter to complete the exercise without fear of losing control of the weight.

steroids (anabolic)   Synthetic derivatives of male hormones that increase the levels of testosterone in the blood, which can cause the development of masculine characteristics in women, such as increased muscularity, deepening of the voice, and increased facial hair. Anabolic steroids are banned by college and professional sports organizations and the International Olympic Committee.

strength   The ability to exert enough force on an object to put it into motion at any speed.

stretching   Exercises designed to loosen up your muscles, ligaments, and joints in preparation for a workout to help prevent injury.

tapering   A training technique in which you gradually lessen the intensity and volume of your workout as you approach a major competition or tournament.

tendons   Fibrous tissue that connects your muscles to your bones.

testosterone   A steroid hormone produced in the body that is responsible for the development and maintenance of male secondary sex characteristics.

toxins   Poisonous substances produced by living cells or organisms that are capable of causing disease when introduced into the body.

training plateau   A point in your training program when you are continuing to train at the same intensity but are realizing little or no gain in power, strength, or muscle size.

triceps   The large muscle running along the back of your upper arm that guides the extension of your forearm.

twitch   The contraction of a muscle that occurs when your nerves send a signal to the muscle that causes the release of the chemical acetylcholine.

uniaxial joint   A joint that allows one type of movement, like a hinge. Your elbow is a uniaxial joint.

universal machine   A type of weight machine that employs a system of wires and pulleys to provide resistance.

vitamins   Fat-soluble or water-soluble organic substances derived from plants and animals that are essential for your body's growth and maintenance.

volume   The number of total repetitions performed during a workout, which can be figured out by multiplying the number of sets times the number of repetitions.

warm-up   Any series of light exercises or stretches that increases blood flow to your muscles before you participate in a workout or competition.

weight belt   A wide belt, made of leather or synthetic material, that is worn by weight lifters to support the lower back and abdomen during lifting.

weight machine   Any machine that provides different types of resistance exercises and allows you to change the amount of resistance. They demand less emphasis on technique and balance than free weights, and are generally easier to use.

wooden dowel   Substitute for a barbell that is used by beginning weight lifters to practice technique.

ASSOCIATIONS/ ORGANIZATIONS

National Strength and Conditioning Association
530 Communications Circle
Suite 204
Colorado Springs, CO 80905
http://www.nsca-lift.org/menu.asp

National Institute for Fitness and Sport
250 University Boulevard
Indianapolis, IN 46202
http://www.nifs.org

American College of Sports Medicine
401 West Michigan Street
Indianapolis, IN 46202-3233
http://www.acsm.org

Bigger Faster Stronger, Inc.
843 West 2400 South
Salt Lake City, UT 84119
http://www.biggerfasterstronger.com

Women's Sports Foundation
Eisenhower Park
East Meadow, NY 11554
http://www.womenssportsfoundation.org

FURTHER READING

Aaberg, Everett. *Muscle Mechanics*. Champaign, Ill.: Human Kinetics Publishing, 1998.

Baechle, Thomas R., ed. *Essentials of Strength Training and Conditioning*. Champaign, Ill.: Human Kinetics Publishing, 1994.

Bompa, Tudor. *Periodization Training for Sports*. Champaign, Ill.: Human Kinetics Publishing, 1999.

Chu, Donald. *Jumping into Plyometrics*. Champaign, Ill.: Human Kinetics Publishing, 1998.

Costello, Frank, and E. J. Kreis. *Sports Agility*. Nashville, Tenn.: Taylor Sports Publishing, 1993.

Faigenbaum, Avery, and Wayne Westcott. *Strength and Power for Young Athletes*. Champaign, Ill.: Human Kinetics Publishing, 2000.

Fleck, Steven J., and William Kraemer. *Periodization Breakthrough!: The Ultimate Training System*. Ronkonkoma, N.Y.: Advanced Research Press, 1996.

Kraemer, William J., and Steven J. Fleck. *Strength Training for Young Athletes*. Champaign, Ill.: Human Kinetics Publishing, 1993.

Radcliffe, James C., and Robert C. Farentinos. *High-Powered Plyometrics*. Champaign, Ill.: Human Kinetics Publishing, 1999.

Shepard, Greg. *Bigger, Faster, Stronger—The Total Program*. Champaign, Ill.: Human Kinetics Publishing, 2003.

INDEX

Boldface page numbers denote major treatment of a topic. Those in *italics* denote illustrations.